The Boy's Book Of Heroes

by

Helena Peake

Double9 BOOKS

The Boy's Book Of Heroes

by Helena Peake

ISBN: 978-93-59952-81-9

Published by

DOUBLE 9 BOOKS
2/13-B, Ansari Road
Daryaganj, New Delhi – 110002
info@double9books.com
www.double9books.com
Tel. 011-40042856

ABOUT THE AUTHOR

Helena Peake is the carried out writer of "The Boy's Book of Heroes," a book that stands as a testament to her dedication to younger readers and the enduring impact of heroic figures during records. Published in 2016, this book is a compelling and inspirational journey via the lives of a number of the arena's maximum first-rate heroes. Peake's writing style in "The Boy's Book of Heroes" is engaging and informative, designed to captivate the imagination of younger readers. Through the tales of each well-known and lesser-regarded heroes, she introduces younger audiences to people who have displayed terrific courage, resilience, and values. The book covers a numerous array of heroes, encompassing figures from various fields and time periods, along with explorers, scientists, activists, and leaders. This complete technique gives young readers with a nicely-rounded know-how of heroism in unique contexts. Helena Peake's "The Boy's Book of Heroes" now not most effective educates however also evokes its readers. It emphasizes the traits that outline heroism, which includes willpower, compassion, and the capacity to make a positive effect on the sector. By doing so, the book encourages young minds to explore their personal capability and the methods wherein they, too, can turn out to be heroes in their own right.

CONTENTS

HEREWARD
LAST OF THE SAXONS

In the days of Edward the Confessor there lived in Mercia a noble Anglo-Saxon youth named Hereward. He was brave, stedfast, and spirited, but so violent and overbearing, so ready to quarrel and to use his sword, if everything he desired was not conceded to him at once that the youths he played and wrestled with around his home at Bourne [1] , resolved to make complaint of him to his father, Leofric, the great Earl of Mercia.

Leofric was a very valiant man, and he had done King Edward good service at the time of Earl Godwin's rebellion. He had three sons; of these Hereward was the second; the eldest was Algar, whom the Confessor made lord over East Anglia.

Leofric was very much grieved when he heard, day after day, of the unruly deeds of his son, and found that he paid little heed to the reproofs he so justly deserved. And if Leofric was grieved, far more so was his wife, the saintly lady Godiva, who passed nearly the whole of her time in the performance of good works, feeding and clothing the poor, nursing the sick, and praying long hours for those she loved, and it may be most of all for her wayward son, Hereward. Besides this, she gave large sums of money for the support of religious houses, and founded the monastery at Coventry, which is said to have contained greater treasure of gold, silver, and jewels, than any other in England.

But father and mother at last were wearied out, and Leofric persuaded King Edward to outlaw his turbulent son, as the only means of preserving peace in the neighbourhood of his castle of Bourne.

The youth, not the least dismayed when sentence was passed upon him, set out on his travels accompanied by one servant, named Martin, as brave and as reckless as himself, and who followed him because he loved him. Perhaps some of his relations were sorry after all to see him go, for they could not help admiring his free, brave spirit, and amongst those who cared for him was his uncle Brand, abbot of Peterborough, a very pious man, as the chroniclers say, but haughty and unbending to the enemies of his land.

Let us glance at Hereward as he bade farewell for many a year to the home of his youth. He was of middle height, broad shouldered, and sturdy limbed, but active and graceful in all his movements. His features were handsome, his golden hair fell in long curls over his shoulders, according to the Saxon fashion; one of his large eyes being blue and the other grey, gave a strange expression to his countenance.

It is supposed that he lived chiefly in the woods and forests during the early days of his exile, but a few months after he quitted Bourne, we find him "beyond Northumberland" with the Fleming, Gilbert of Ghent, who bore him good-will, and had sent for him as soon as he heard that he was outlawed. Hereward had not been long in his friend's house, which was in some part of Scotland, when an event occurred which redounded very much to his credit.

It was the custom then for rich men to have various kinds of sports at Christmas, Easter, and Whitsuntide, and they used to keep a number of wild beasts in enclosures, which were led forth at these seasons, that the noble youths assembled might try their strength against them.

It was Christmas time when Hereward arrived "beyond Northumberland." He had passed some joyous days hunting in the wintry forests, and had become a great favourite with the company, because he excelled in all manly sports, and could charm the ladies besides by singing sweetly, and playing on the harp, in the long winter evenings. But when he looked at the wild beasts in their cages, he only saw one that he thought he should like to fight with, and that was a huge white bear, which was known to be exceedingly fierce. And beyond this it was said that its parent was the famed Norwegian bear, which lived far away in the pine woods of the north, and, according to the fable believed in at the time, was endowed with human sense, and could understand human speech.

Now it happened one day that the white bear broke the bars of its enclosure, and rushed out, killing and tearing to pieces all the animals that came in its path. This must have been very alarming, and worse still, it was making its way towards a room, opening out of the court where the women and children belonging to the house had taken refuge, and some knights in their terror had followed them, instead of trying to drive back the fierce creature with their lances. Hereward had just come in from hunting, and saw at a glance what had happened; he went straight up to the bear, and thrusting his sword through its head, he laid it dead on the ground.

His praises after this were sung far and wide; but amidst all the joy there was a secret plot made to destroy him by some of the knights who had shown themselves to be cowards, and were jealous of the bold deed he had performed. So one day they concealed themselves in the wood and tried to kill him as he came slowly along the mossy paths followed by his servant Martin. The story tells how Hereward slew two of these knights in self-defence, and another crept away, or was carried wounded to the house. Soon after this he bade Gilbert of Ghent farewell; he said that he could not live happily where there were traitors, but those who loved him were grieved when he rode away, and the women shed many tears, remembering how he had saved them with his strong right arm from a cruel death.

From Scotland he went to Cornwall, and there we are told he performed some brave deeds, and rescued a Cornish princess by slaying in combat a fierce and cruel Pict, a giant in height, whom her father had commanded her to marry against her own inclination.

Some time after he was heard of in Ireland, where he took part in the warlike exploits of King Ranald. Whenever there was fighting he was sure to be found where the danger was thickest, and the name of "The Wake" was given to him because he was always on the watch for his enemies, and could never be taken unawares.

But in Ireland he began to get homesick; he longed to see his brave father once more, and his mother, the Lady of Bourne, sitting amongst her maidens, or gliding amongst the sick like some comforting angel; he wanted to know if his relations had any kindly feeling left towards him. This longing became so strong that he asked the king to give him two ships, which Ranald granted him readily in return for his services, and with these he set out for England. But he had not sailors enough on board, and since he could get no more to serve him in Ireland, he sailed up northwards towards the Orkneys. When he reached these islands a storm arose and one of his ships was wrecked on the shore of Hoy.

With the other vessel he hoped to get safe to England, but he had not been long at sea when the winds blew furiously, the waves dashed and foamed, and storm-tossed for many days he was at last driven on the shore of Flanders. In this country he found a welcome, and married a noble Flemish lady named Torfrida. No part of his life, perhaps, was more peaceful than that which he spent in his new home: nevertheless, it appears that wherever he was, he always engaged in the wars that were carried on around him, and never failed to distinguish himself by his valour.

Whilst Hereward had been wandering about all this time an outlaw, great changes had taken place in the affairs of England. On the death of Edward the Confessor the English had welcomed Harold, son of Earl Godwin to the throne, quietly setting aside Edgar Atheling, who was too weak-minded to defend his right, or to have ruled had he been king. But

Harold had scarcely been crowned when William of Normandy began making his vast preparations for the conquest of England. The terrible battle of Hastings had been fought; Harold the Second was slain, and nearly all the bravest warriors amongst the English had fallen on the battle-field. And with the exception of a few valiant noblemen, it seemed as if the people of England had lost all spirit and would bow quietly to the Norman yoke. Leofric of Mercia was dead; Algar also had died, leaving two fair young sons, Edwin and Morcar, who at the time of the conquest were accounted the most powerful noblemen in the land, Edwin being Earl of Mercia, and Morcar, Earl of Northumberland. It must be remembered that Mercia included all the midland counties of England.

The brothers proclaimed Edgar Atheling king, and tried to persuade the Londoners to rise; but their efforts were of no avail, and they were soon obliged to retire to their own lands.

One day, some emigrants came to Flanders and told Hereward all that had happened in England. Oh, how he wished he had been amongst the Saxons on the day of battle! Surely, if there had been many as brave and stern as he, the Normans would have been driven back. And when he learned that some Frenchmen had taken possession of the estate of Bourne, which was now his own, and that they were cruelly oppressing his widowed mother, he only waited to bid Torfrida farewell, and then set out for England, followed by Martin, with the intention of avenging his mother's wrongs.

It was late in the evening when he drew near the old house of Bourne. Some of the companions of his boyhood recognised him, and told him that William of Normandy had given his estate to a low-born foreigner, and that a party of Normans had just taken up their abode in the house. So Hereward hastened on towards Bourne, and sought out a house at the end of the long street which belonged to one Percy where he thought he could lodge for the night. Here he found a number of fighting men bewailing the misfortunes of England, and heard from them how the Frenchmen had robbed his mother of all her treasures, and how his youngest brother, a youth of sixteen, had been slain defending her, and his head had been fastened up over the door of the house. And one amongst the company of warriors said, that if Hereward, the outlawed son of Leofric had been at home, this trouble would never have come upon Bourne.

Now Hereward, having formed a plan in his mind, did not make himself known yet: he only said that he had come from Flanders, but the men perceived by the flash of his eye and his proud bearing that his spirit was kindled at their wrongs, and their hearts leaned towards him because he looked so brave and strong.

After a while, the warriors dropped off one by one to sleep as the night wore on. Hereward heard in the silence around, the sound of harps and joyful singing, and the clinking of goblets. He asked a boy what it was that he heard, and the boy said it was the merry-making of the guests in the lord's house above, where the youngest son had been killed only the day before. Then Hereward beckoned Martin and Percy to him, and by their means he covered his helmet and his shining coat of mail with some woman's robe of black stuff, and went out with Martin, who was disguised in like manner, to the house of Bourne. The first grievous sight that awaited him was the head of his young brother fixed up above the door. He could see through the windows the Normans sitting at their feast in noisy merriment: they boasted loudly of their deeds, and spoke slightingly of Hereward, whom they believed to be far away in Flanders, although one Flemish woman amongst the guests declared that if he had been there he could have overthrown them all.

Then Hereward, the Wake, the Terrible, waited to hear no more; he rushed with Martin on those unprepared men; a fearful struggle began, and of all the foreigners, it is said that not one was left there alive when the day dawned. Such is the story told by the Monk of Ely, of the fierce and relentless manner in which Bourne was rescued from the Normans.

The Lady Godiva was very thankful to know that she had yet a son to protect her. After this night of horror she removed to the Abbey of Croyland, where she lived praying and fasting, and tending the poor and sick until she died.

In the year 1069 there was a rebellion throughout England. The English were angry and indignant when they saw how the Conqueror bestowed all the high offices in the land upon his Normans, whilst he trod their own liberties under foot.

Several bands of patriots assembled in the marshy lands of Cambridgeshire, and there in the island of Ely they formed entrenchments of earth and wood, and lived in security, often completely hidden by the mists that rose up from the stagnant waters. There, too, they were amongst friends; the Abbey of Croyland was in the marshes; Peterborough was not far off northward, and as yet the monastery was held by the Abbot Brand, who prided himself on never having sought favour from the Conqueror.

Meanwhile, Hereward had returned to Flanders, but he did not remain there long, and when he came back to England a second time, bringing with him his wife Torfrida and his little daughter, his kinsmen welcomed him heartily, and asked him to lead them in the battles they hoped to fight with the Normans.

But notwithstanding the numerous warlike deeds he had performed, he was not what was called a legitimate "miles" or knight, and to be this it was requisite that he should receive knighthood according to the Anglo-Saxon custom. It was a law that every man desiring to be a lawful knight should go to some abbey, and the evening before the ceremony of knighthood was to take place, should confess his sins in deep penitence, and pass the whole night inside the church in prayer and mortification. The next morning he was to hear mass, and then offer up his sword upon the altar; this being done the Gospel would be read, and the priest, having consecrated the sword, would place it on the neck of the warrior with his blessing. [2]

The Normans looked with much scorn on this manner of knighthood at the hands of a priest, but it may have been, as a modern French historian observes, that they did not like to see so many knights continually rising up amongst a people they had conquered.

Hereward went to Peterborough, [3] with two of his band, Winter and Gwenoch, and persuaded his uncle to knight them all. And he told him that William had given the abbey to Thorold, called "the fighting monk," but that Brand would not believe for a long time.

All the brave Anglo-Saxons rose up now to make a last effort to deliver themselves from the Normans. The Danes came to help them under Objorn, brother of Sweyn, King of Norway. Edgar Atheling appeared from Scotland with a number of brave men. The people of York put their Norman governor to death; the fiercest struggles were in the north of England. Hereward established himself with his followers in the island of Ely, and had a fortress of wood constructed which served them for shelter, and was a point where other men of like mind could meet them from the forests and fastnesses around. And here they remained for a long time to the great annoyance of the Normans who could not reach them because their horses constantly lost their footing in the marshes and bogs around.

Thorold set out for Peterborough, but Brand did not live to be despoiled of his abbey. Hereward hearing that the fighting monk was coming, hastened to Peterborough with some of his men, and when they found that the monks were not at all inclined to bar the entrance of Thorold, they took all the crosses, and golden cups, the sacred robes and staffs belonging to the abbey, and carried them to their quarters in Ely. And soon after this the monks of Peterborough opened the gates to the Normans.

The Danish warriors made their way to Ely, but William found means to persuade Sweyn to recall them, and he bribed Objorn to retire by giving him large presents and the liberty of plundering the sea coast. The departure of the Danes caused great vexation to the people in Ely, because they carried away with them all the sacred treasures of Peterborough.

Now Taillebois, the Angevin, [4] had many followers, and being a great boaster, he swore that he would quickly drive the outlaws out of their hiding places. The fighting monk was out in the marshes, and he told him that he meant to attack the English. Hereward let him enter a forest of willows which served to protect the patriots from their enemies, but as Taillebois went in on one side of the forest, he came out on the other side himself, and falling upon Thorold and his men, who had remained behind, he took them all prisoners and kept them in the marshes, not releasing the abbot until he had paid him three thousand marks of silver.

The young brothers, Edwin and Morcar, had not joined in this last rebellion, but they were not at all happy at King William's court; their hearts were with their brave kinsman and not with the conqueror of their land. At last Edwin went to Northumberland to lay his plans for another rising, and Morcar fled to the island of Ely, where Hereward was still holding out bravely, although the Saxon nobles in other parts of England had all given way.

William was very uneasy so long as he could not gain possession of Ely. In the hope of preventing the Saxons from coming out of the island, he surrounded it with flat-bottomed boats and made a causeway to the extent of two miles. The workmen who were employed in constructing the causeway were much harassed by Hereward and his men, and the king was persuaded by some of his nobles to place an old woman, believed to be a witch, in a wooden tower at the head of the works that she might use her spells against the enemy. Hereward, on this, came out with his troop and set fire to the willows that grew closely around the tower, and thus the poor old woman perished in the flames. This seems to have been a very cruel act on the part of our hero, although, unhappily, in those days, the burning of witches was not considered a crime.

The island remained blockaded for several months. At last the inmates of a monastery in the interior got very hungry because no provisions could be brought in, and they sent word to the king that they would show him how his troops might enter the island if he would promise not to deprive them of their property. Two Norman knights, Gilbert de Clare, and Guillaume de Larenne undertook to try the path; the king's troops poured in after them, and it is said that they put a thousand Englishmen to the sword. All the nobles now surrendered except Hereward, and William imprisoned Morcar, and Egelwine, Bishop of Durham, who had taken refuge in Ely. Morcar died in his prison, [5] and Egelwine went mad, and as for the others "they suffered so much in their captivity that it had been better for them if they had been put to death the day they were taken." [6]

Hereward, with a few of his men, fought his way through the enemy and escaped from their pursuit by difficult paths to the lowlands of Lincolnshire. There some Saxon fishermen who were in the habit of carrying fish every day to the Norman stations, along the marshes, concealed them in their boats by covering them up with straw. When the boats reached one of these strongholds, the Normans little imagining that their greatest enemy was so near, purchased their fish as usual, and when it was cooked, sat down to dinner. They had scarcely begun to eat when Hereward and his men rose up out of the straw, and with hatchets in their hands rushed suddenly upon them. There was a fierce conflict, and many of the Normans were slain; those who survived fled in great terror and left their horses behind them ready saddled. Then Hereward, and the followers that remained to him, each chose a good steed for himself and galloped away into the forests.

In the country around they found many friends, and before they came as far as Huntingdon their company included a hundred well armed men, all of them faithful subjects of Hereward and proud to share his exploits. Their numbers increasing daily, they became so strong at last that Gaimar, the French poet, says they might have assailed a city. And a very strong castle they did take, and found in it quantities of gold, silver, and armour, besides rich furs and stuffs. So for a while they went on fighting under their brave leader with spirit unquenched; often one Englishman against three of the enemy.

But hope died out even in the heart of Hereward when the power of the Conqueror became fully established in the land. His friends were either dead or in prison, or they had been sent blinded and maimed to their homes. The persuasions of a Saxon lady, named Alfrueda, helped to induce him to make peace, or rather a truce, with William, and he set out accordingly, followed by three of his comrades, for Winchester, where the king was then living. But when he drew near the gates of the city, he thought that this manner of presenting himself before his sovereign was unworthy of his own high rank, and he turned back in order to provide a more dignified escort. The second time he approached Winchester he was at the head of forty men, all clad in armour from head to foot, and mounted on handsomely accoutred horses. The king had a great admiration for the valour and constancy of Hereward;

he welcomed him gladly to his court, and suffered him to retain his estate at Bourne.

Notwithstanding this, the Normans were always trying to quarrel with the brave Saxon, and one day Oger, the Breton, offended him so deeply that a combat took place between them, in which Oger was wounded. Then the enemies of Hereward told the king that he had spoken evil of him, and persuaded him to arrest him for that and for having wounded Oger. William seems to have been very ready to believe ill of his powerful subject, and ordered him to be imprisoned in Bedford Castle, where he remained a whole year.

When Hereward was released he went to live in his house at Bourne, and was known by the name of "the Lord of the Fens." The monk who wrote his life in Latin, asserts that he died peacefully in his home, but other documents have been found which prove that he did not meet his death in quiet, but in fierce conflict with his enemies.

His house at Bourne was frequently attacked by the Normans. One day he was sitting outside the door, the weather was sultry, and he had fallen asleep. Suddenly, he was awakened by the clash of weapons and the tread of horses, and found that he was surrounded by a party of Bretons. He was without his coat of mail, and had only a sword and a short pike. Undaunted amongst so many, he snatched up a shield that was lying near, and defended himself "like a lion." Taillebois, his greatest enemy, was with the troop. When he perceived him he cried out that they were all traitors because he had made his peace with the king, and that if they sought his life or his goods they should pay dearly for either. Terrible was the struggle that ensued; the Normans fell around; Hereward himself received four sword thrusts at once; it was Raoul de Dol, a Breton knight, who rushed forward to give him the death blow; then, he made one last effort, and flinging his shield in the face of his foe, he fell back dead.

The life of Hereward was marked by many fierce deeds, and would that all anger and strife had been hushed before he died! His memory must be cherished because he loved his country so well, and it was great and noble of him, when all his partizans had laid down their arms in submission, to stand up alone in her righteous cause, and to be the last man to yield to the thraldom of a conqueror.

The daughter of Hereward was given in marriage by William to a valiant knight named Hugh de Evermere, to whom she brought the lands of Bourne. Torfrida ended her days in the Abbey of Croyland.

FOOTNOTES:

[1] Bourne, then called Brun, in Lincolnshire.

[2] See Sharon Turner.

[3] Peterborough was formerly called Burgh.

[4] Angevin, a native of Anjou.

[5] See Gaimar.

[6] Edwin, the brother of Morcar, was slain by some of his own followers.

THE CID

According to the Spanish chronicles the famous Rodrigo Diaz de Bivar, known by the name of the Cid, was born about the year 1026, in the city of Burgos, the capital of old Castille. His father, Diego Laynez, was descended from Layn Calvo, one of two judges by whom the country was governed after Ordono, its king, had behaved very treacherously. When we first hear of Rodrigo as a youth of gentle manners, but of great courage and bodily strength, Don Ferrando, a Christian king, who traced his descent from the other judge, was ruling over Castille.

Spain was then composed of many different kingdoms; the Moors had been steadily gaining ground ever since they first set foot in the land, more than three hundred years before, whilst the Christians had been trying as steadily to keep them back. Now they held sway over by far the larger portion of Spain; several of the great-cities, especially those in the south, were under the dominion of Moorish kings, and were filled with beautiful buildings, many of which remain, to show what wonderful skill the Arabian architects must have possessed. The Moors lived in great splendour; their palaces and courts were paved with marble, and the walls were covered with arabesques in brilliant colours, or fretwork in gold [7] ; the ceilings were often of cedar wood, inlaid with silver, ivory, or mother of pearl, and the chambers were filled with the fragrance of costly spices, which were kept always burning. Then they had beautiful gardens blooming with roses and myrtles, where orange trees grew, and silvery fountains played into basins of white marble. The outside of their buildings was also richly ornamented, and sometimes with the strangest devices. The Alhambra, the finest of all the Moorish palaces, which still remains in its ancient splendour, was not built in the city of Granada until nearly two hundred years after the death of the Cid.

The Spaniards themselves were very brave, and inherited their valour from the Visigoths, who were in possession of Spain for a long time before the Moors crossed over the sea from Africa. The middle ages were not as dark for them as they were for the other nations of Europe, because their Moorish invaders taught them many useful arts and sciences, and also introduced into Spain various fruits and trees which had hitherto only grown in the East, or in Africa. Amongst these was the pomegranate, with its shining dark green leaves, its beautiful crimson blossom, and its red, juicy fruit; then there was the palm-tree, which was cultivated in the fertile soil of Valencia, until it reached the height of a hundred and fifty feet; and the strange-looking carob-tree, with leaves gloomily dark, and pods full of a sweet pulp, like manna in taste, which were given to the horses and mules.

Some of the Moorish kings were merciful rulers, and rendered their subjects happy; still, as they were strangers and infidels, it was very natural for the Spaniards to wish to drive them out of the land, and Rodrigo de Bivar is renowned for having regained more ground from them than any of the other great Spanish captains.

Whilst Rodrigo was still a youth, a quarrel arose between his father and a certain Count Gomez, during which the Count gave his adversary a blow. Laynez was old and feeble, and could not lift his sword, and he grieved over the insult with a Spaniard's sense of shame and thirst for revenge. Rodrigo, indignant at seeing his father treated thus scornfully, went out and defied the Count to a combat, and slew him in the struggle. And when he came home and told his father how he had avenged the affront that had been offered him, the old man decreed that he should be considered thenceforth as the head of the house of Layn Calvo. Alas! those were terrible times when men fired up at the slightest provocation, and thought their honour was at stake if an offence were not wiped out with the shedding of blood, and seldom or never gave the "soft answer that turneth away wrath."

A little while after this, the Moors, led by five of their kings, entered Castille; they plundered the cities and carried away captive men, women, and children, besides seizing the cows and the sheep that were feeding in the pastures. They were going home in triumph when Rodrigo, young as he was, came up with them in the mountains of Oca, and put them all to the rout.

> "He rode to the hills of Oca, where the Moormen lay,
> He conquered all the Moors, and took from their prey."

His father being now dead, he went home to his mother, a noble lady, the daughter of the Count of Asturias, and told her how he had won back all that the Moors had taken, and had made their five kings captive. His mother was very proud of his success, and rejoiced still more when she heard him say that it would not be fair to keep the kings in prison, and that he would send them all back to their own territory. And the Moors were so touched by his generous conduct towards them that they resolved to pay tribute and to remain subject to the king of Castille.

The next event recorded in his life is his marriage with Ximena, daughter of Count Gomez, whom he had slain. It is said that Ximena, without any regard for the memory of her father, went to the king, Don Ferrando, and entreated him to allow her to be married to Rodrigo de Bivar, because she thought that he would one day be the richest and most powerful man in the realm.

The marriage took place, and a short time after, Don Ferrando, of Castille, and Don Ramiero, of Arragon, had a quarrel about a city called Calahorra, each laying claim to it as his rightful possession. As it seemed impossible to find out which king had the right on his side, it was agreed to decide the question by single combat, so Don Martin Gonzalez, accounted the bravest knight in all Spain, was chosen to fight for Ramiero, and Rodrigo de Bivar was to fight for Ferrando.

Before the day of the combat arrived, Rodrigo set out on a pilgrimage to the holy shrine of St. James, at Compostella, accompanied by twenty knights. The Spaniards have a curious legend in reference to this journey which must not be passed over, although so many strange stories are told of the Cid that it is difficult to discover how many of the events detailed in his life are really true.

On the road to Compostella the pilgrims found a leper struggling in a quagmire, and crying in vain for help. Rodrigo hastened to his relief and dragged him out of the muddy water. Then he set him before him on his own horse and continued his journey. When they arrived at the inn where they were to pass the night, Rodrigo seated the leper at supper next himself, and eat with him of all the viands that were served before them off the same plate. The knights to show their disgust at this, rose with one accord and left the supper room. Nevertheless, Rodrigo, feeling sure that no one else in the inn would have pity upon the poor leper or give him shelter, made him share his bed, but when he awoke at midnight he found him gone. After a while a figure appeared before him, clad in shining white garments, and a voice asked him if he were asleep or awake. "I am awake," replied Rodrigo, "but who art thou, and whence is this fragrance and brightness?"

The strange visitant, answered, "I am Saint Lazarus, the leper whom thou hast succoured and honoured for the love of God;" and he told him that when he felt a breath near him, such as he had felt that night, before he appeared, it would be a sign that he should succeed in whatever enterprise he was engaged in at the time; and he told him also that he should be feared both by Christians and Moors, and that his foes should never prevail against him. Then the saint vanished, and Rodrigo, wondering at the extraordinary vision, knelt down, and remained many hours in prayer, and at daybreak he set out on his pilgrimage once more, doing all the good he could along his journey.

On the day fixed for the combat, Rodrigo had not appeared at the spot where it was to take place, and his cousin Alvar Fanez, was preparing to fight in his stead. But at the very moment when the contest was to begin, he stepped forward and took his stand against the champion of Arragon. They fought so fiercely that their lances were broken, and they were both severely wounded, and although Gonzalez taunted his opponent by saying that he should never go back alive to his bride, Doña Ximena, Rodrigo was more cruel to him than he need have been, and gave him his death wound as he lay, faint from loss of blood, upon the ground. Then Don Ferrando came up and embraced Rodrigo, and helped to unharm him himself; he was so glad that he could take possession of Calahorra, but all the people of Arragon sorrowed bitterly for the loss of Gonzalez, their bravest knight.

The Counts of Castille now grew jealous of Rodrigo's renown, and plotted with the Moors that a battle should take place, in which they hoped he might be killed and so stand no longer in their way. The affair was made known to the Moors who were his vassals; they refused to share in the treason, and revealed the whole plot to their lord. The king was very angry when he heard of the treachery of his nobles, and to punish them, he ordered all the traitors to quit the kingdom at once.

About this time Rodrigo was knighted in the great mosque of Coimbra, the king giving him his sword, the queen his horse, and the infanta fastening on his spurs. After this he was called Ruy Diaz, Ruy being short for Rodrigo; and his Moorish vassals when they brought him tribute called him "El Seid," the Arabic for "the lord," so that he was known thenceforth by the name of the Cid.

Not long after this Don Ferrando died, leaving his dominions divided amongst his five children. Sancho had Castille, Alonzo Leon, Garcia Gallicia, and their two sisters, the cities of Tora and Zamora. The brothers kept at peace for only two years, and then they went to war with one another. The Cid remained faithful to the fortunes of Don Sancho, and one day during the war, when the king was being carried away prisoner by thirteen knights who were on the side of Alonzo, Ruy Diaz chanced to come up with them in time, and being unarmed, he asked them to give him a lance. The knights refused at first, but afterwards gave him one, laughing at the idea that one man could hold out against so many. They soon found that they were mistaken, for the Cid overthrew them one after another until only two were left, and thus freed Don Sancho from the power of his enemies. The war between the brothers unhappily lasted some years, and at last Alonzo was defeated by Sancho, and shut up in prison, whence he contrived to escape to the court of the Moorish kings. Sancho himself received a death blow from an unknown hand at the siege of Zamora. Before he died he prayed that his brother Alonzo might come from the land of the Moors and show favour to the Cid, and that the hidalgos would entreat him to forgive whatever wrongs, he, Don Sancho, had done to him.

Alonzo returned from the land of the Moors, and as soon as he arrived his sister Urraca sent letters to all the nobles in the kingdom that they might render him homage. Those of Leon and Gallicia were very glad to come and receive him for their king; then the Castillians appeared, and they kissed his hands, all except the Cid; but they were not all content, for Alonzo had been suspected of having connived at the death of Don Sancho.

When the king saw that the Cid would not kiss his hand, he was vexed, and he asked him why he held back. And the Cid replied that he would never render him homage until he had sworn with twelve of his hidalgos who were likewise suspected, that he had not connived at the death of Don Sancho.

The king consented to take the oath in the great church of Saint Gadea, in Burgos, and went thither on the appointed day with his sisters and all his court. The Cid made him stand with the hidalgos on a high stage so that they might be seen by all the people in the church; then he took the book of the holy gospels and laid it on the altar, and when Alonzo had placed his hand upon it, he asked him in the most solemn manner if he had anything to do with his brother's death. And he said that if it were so, and he denied the crime, he should die a like death himself, at the hands of one who was not a Castillian, but would come from a strange land.

At the end of every sentence the Cid spoke, the king and his hidalgos answered, Amen.

It was an awful scene, and when Alonzo heard the doom pronounced upon him if he did not speak the truth, he turned pale, and asked Ruy Diaz why he pressed him so much, because he made him take the oath three times. When he had sworn that he was innocent for the last time, the Cid kissed his hand and acknowledged him for his king, and from thenceforth Alonzo reigned over Castille, Leon, Gallicia, and Navarre, and was free from the attempts of his brother Garcia since he had invited him to his court, and then shut him up in a strong castle, where he remained to the end of his days. It was a very long time, however, before he could look kindly on the Cid, for he thought he had done him a great injury by making him take the oath so many times before his people.

The first expedition of Ruy Diaz after this was against the kings of Seville and Cordova, in which he won great honour, and afterwards returned to Castille laden with spoils. Then he lay sick for a long time, and could not go with Alonzo to fight the Moors in another part of Spain. And it happened that when the king was far away, a vast company of Moors, thinking that all was quiet, entered Castille and did great damage to the country. The Cid, hearing of this, roused himself and gathered his strength and pursued them as far as the city of Toledo. The Castillians around Toledo were very jealous of his power, and they complained to Alonzo that Ruy Diaz had driven the Moors into their territory on purpose to annoy them.

Alonzo flew into a great passion, and summoned the Cid to his presence, and glad of an opportunity of vexing him, ordered him to leave the country of Castille for ever, and all the fair domains he possessed.

When the sentence was passed the Cid's cousin, Alvar Fanez, and all his friends, kinsmen, and vassals, declared that if he must needs quit the land they would follow him into his exile and remain faithful to him all the days of their life. This comforted Ruy Diaz, although he did not desire that so many of those he loved should condemn themselves to wander in the land of the Moors for his sake. He sent his wife Ximena, and his two little daughters, Elvira and Sol, [8] to the convent of Saint Peter, of Cardeña, where they would be safe; and one sad day he bade farewell to his home in Castille and set out on his wanderings, the king having granted him nine days for his journey out of the country.

The costly furniture of his palace in Burgos had been all stored away; there were no people coming and going; no voices of children gladdened the empty halls; the birds were all gone from the perches, there would be no more pleasant pastime of hawking, the whole place was silent and desolate.

When the Cid saw this he knelt down and turned towards the east, and prayed that he might be victorious over the Moors, and gain enough to requite his friends for their devotion. Then he turned to the whole company and cheered them with the hope that he might yet be able to return to Castille in honour. And an old woman, who stood by the door, repeated the Spanish proverb, "Go in a lucky moment, and you shall make spoil of whatever you desire."

The mausoleum of the Cid now occupies the spot where his palace stood, and his statue ornaments the gate of Saint Maria, which is the principal entrance into the city of Burgos, and opens on to one of the bridges leading out into the suburb called Vega.

As Ruy Diaz came with his people through the streets of Burgos, the citizens wept aloud; they were so grieved to see him depart, and to know that no house might afford him shelter even for one night. So when the dark came he was obliged to have a tent raised on the sandy plain and rest for a while there.

At last he got to the convent of Cardeña, and bade a long farewell to his wife and daughters, giving them a hundred marks of gold for their expenditure; and before he left he gave the Abbot fifty marks of silver, and commended his family to his care, for he did not feel sure that he should ever see them again. Then he pursued his journey, travelling all night because he had a long and difficult way to go before he could get to the land of the Moors. The next day but one they crossed the river Douro in wooden boats, and rested at a place called Figueruela. And there in the night he either dreamed or had a vision of an angel coming to him who said, "Cid, be of good cheer, for it shall be well with thee all thy life long; and thou shalt accomplish all that thou shalt undertake, and shalt become rich and honoured." The Cid thought very much on what he had heard, and he arose and gave thanks for the mercy that had befallen him. The following day he reached the wild Sierra, of Miedes, and he said, "Friends, let us mount our horses quickly, and cross the Sierra and go out of the kingdom of Don Alonzo, for this is the ninth day, and it is time we were gone." So they passed the Sierra in the dark night and then they were in the country of the Moors. The whole company of the Cid amounted to 400 horsemen, and 3,000 foot. They travelled by night, and hid by day until they reached the Castle of Castregon. Ruy Diaz concealed himself and his friends close by, and in the morning the Moors, not knowing they were there, came out of the Castle gates to go to their work; the Spaniards rushed suddenly upon them, slaying some and dispersing the rest, and soon got possession of the castle where they found a quantity of gold and silver. But they could not stay in it because there was no water, and besides this, the Moors all around were vassals of Don Alonzo. So the Cid left the Moors there whom he had taken prisoner in the skirmish, and went further on his way to meet with fresh adventures. During the whole time of his exile he remained loyal to the king who had so unjustly treated him, and did him good service, for he took many strong castles from the Moors, and either drove the invaders out of the land or made them subject to Castille. He shared with his company all the rich spoils he won, and after many brave exploits determined to send his cousin Alvar to Alonzo with a present of thirty Arab horses, and a message entreating him to restore him to his favour, and to give back to his friends the estates they had lost by following him into his exile.

When the king saw the beautiful Arab horses, each with a fine sword mounted in silver hanging from its saddle, his face brightened, and he could not bring himself to refuse the gift. Still he thought it was too soon yet to pardon the mighty Cid, and only restored to his friends and relations their lands.

Ruy Diaz got as far as the district of Ternel in Arragon, and there he settled himself in a fortress on a high rock which has been called ever since "The Rock of the Cid." From this stronghold he sallied forth from time to time against the Moors, and forced numbers of them to pay tribute. And besides overcoming the Moors, he served the king by punishing some great Spanish lords who had been guilty of treason, and Alonzo at last desired him to return to the court. The Cid waited yet to take the strong Castle of Rueda from the Moors, and then he came back to Castille in honour, as he had hoped on the sorrowful day when he left Burgos. All the king's displeasure passed away when Ruy Diaz came before him and delivered into his hands the rich treasures he had captured, and Alonzo gave him many castles, and the right of keeping in future all the places he should win from the Moors for himself.

Ruy Diaz was chosen to lead the Spanish army against Toledo in the year 1032. This city was possessed by the Moorish king Yahia, and was considered so important a place, that all the Christian sovereigns in Spain made up their quarrels, and joined together to besiege it. Yahia held out for three years, and then only yielded up the city on condition that he should reign over Valencia instead. The first Christian banner that entered Toledo was the banner of the Cid. A story is told by the Spaniards how, when the army had to cross a ford of the Tagus, that they might get nearer the city, and the river was so swollen that the horsemen feared to plunge into it, a monk of the order of St. Benedict rode over first on an ass, after which the whole army passed over in safety.

Later on, Castille was threatened by the Almoravides, a nation of African Moors. The Moorish kings already settled in Spain had many bitter quarrels amongst themselves; there was trouble and treason all over the land. Yahia, who was protected by the Cid, and called himself his friend, was murdered by a wicked alcayde named Abeniaf soon after he had joined with Ruy Diaz to defend Spain against the Almoravides. Abeniaf buried the treasures of the murdered king, and let some of the new invaders into Valencia, for which service they made him Wali, or governor of the city.

The Cid came with a great army of Christians and Moors, and lay siege to Valencia, so incensed was he at the cruel death of Yahia, and began by attacking the suburbs, because by gaining them he could close all round the city, and prevent the Moors from going in or coming out. That siege of Valencia was very terrible, the people died daily of hunger; they eat horses, dogs, cats, and mice, and when all the flesh was gone they had only a little wheat and garlic, and a few raisins and figs.

In their sore need they implored some more of the Almoravides to come to their aid, although a great quarrel had broken out between that people and Abeniaf. The Almoravides set out for Valencia, but they were dismayed by a violent tempest which arose and turned back. Then the besieged went almost mad through hunger and misery, and the Cid came nearer its walls, thinking that famine would force them to yield. The longer the siege lasted, the more defiant did Abeniaf become; besides which he governed the people very cruelly, and oppressed them in every way. The Cid was very cruel too outside their walls, and showed them no mercy. He sent word to them that he would burn all persons who should dare to come out of the city, and it is said that several Moors who tried to escape were burned by his command. Many men, women, and children, too, came out whenever the gates were opened, and sold themselves to the Christians for food. The price of a Moor was a loaf and a pitcher of wine.

At last Abeniaf agreed to deliver up the place if no succour came within fifteen days, provided he might still continue in his office of Wali. The people thought they might yet be saved, because they had entreated the King of Saragossa to assist them, but no help came, and the gates were opened, and the Christians poured in to the city.

The Cid entered with all the hidalgos and knights, and went up to the highest tower in the wall, whence he could look down on the whole of Valencia; and the Moors came to him, and they kissed his hands, and bade him welcome. The Cid, in return, ordered that all the windows of the tower which looked towards the streets should be closed, that the Spaniards might not annoy the Moors by prying into their affairs, and commanded the Christians to guard the people and to pay them the greatest honour. The Moors were very grateful for his kindness, and rejoiced indeed that the city had been given up, for now the provision merchants could come inside the gates and they could buy food; and some of them were so famished that they went and plucked the grass and herbs from the field, and tried thus to satisfy their sharp hunger. It must have been a sad sight to have seen those who had survived the famine standing about like ghosts, whilst there was mourning in every house, and space had not been found to bury all the dead.

The Cid planted his banner on the Alcazar, which was the name given to all royal houses and palaces in Spain. He caused Abeniaf to be seized by force, and after he had made him say where he had concealed the treasures of Yahia he condemned him to be burnt alive, but showed mercy to his son when the Moors entreated him not to include him in the punishment of his father; and had the Cid put the innocent child to death it would have been as dreadful a crime as Abeniaf was guilty of in murdering Yahia.

The city of Valencia lay in a great plain which was called the Garden, because it was covered with the most luxuriant vegetation, and trees, such as the mulberry, olive, orange, carob, and palm grew in its fertile soil. There were fair gardens lying between the walls and the shore.

When the Cid had taken up his abode in the vast and beautiful Alcazar, the people began to cast off their sorrow and gloom, and to take part in the rejoicings made by the Spaniards. Valencia was now all his own. He suffered the Moors to remain in the city and to keep all their herds and flocks; they were to give him a tenth part of their substance, and to retain all their customs; and he made a good man Wali over them that they might be governed by their own laws. Those who were not content with this arrangement, he ordered to go and dwell in the suburb of Alcudia, outside the walls. From this time he was called the Cid Campeador, the latter title being given to one greatly renowned for his exploits.

One day, Hieronymo, a holy and learned man, "all shaven and shorn," came from the East to Valencia, and desired to see the Cid. He said that if he might once meet the Moors on the battle-field, and have his fill of smiting them, he would be content. These were warlike words for a priest, but they pleased Ruy Diaz, and the very next day after the stranger arrived the mosques were changed into churches, and Hieronymo was made Bishop of Valencia.

The King of Seville soon came with the Almoravides to besiege the Cid in his new abode. Ruy Diaz defeated him, and won from them his famed horse Bavieca, although the chronicles say that Bavieca was the horse he chose when a boy, because it was so fiery, and the name was given to it from his godfather exclaiming, "Bavieca (meaning simpleton) thou hast chosen ill."

After this he sent his faithful cousin Alvar with a number of brave knights to fetch his wife and daughters from the convent of Cardeña, where they had been all this time. The ladies were joyful indeed to hear that Valencia was gained, and when they drew near, the Cid came out on his horse Bavieca, with a stately company to meet them, and he took them up to the highest tower of the Alcazar, whence they could see all the fair city lying in its plain beside the sea, and its beautiful houses built by the Moorish architects, its fountains and gateways, and its gardens filled with the brilliant flowers and luscious fruits of the East.

Doña Ximena and her daughters had been in Valencia about three months, when news was brought to the Cid that King Yusef was coming from Morocco with 50,000 horsemen, and myriads of men on foot, to invest the city by sea and land. The Campeador was not alarmed; he had his fortresses well manned, and the enormously thick walls of the city repaired, and he got in plenty of provisions, whilst a number of his vassals, Christians and Moors, came to his aid.

The day before the battle he took his wife and Elvira and Sol to the tower, and showed them the Moors as they gained their footing on shore. Soon they began to enter the gardens, and Ruy Diaz told a very brave man to go down thither with two hundred knights, and show them a little play. So he went down, and soon drove them out of the gardens. The Cid, being so often at war, had certain signals, by which the knights knew how many of them were to arm themselves and assemble, the signal being usually the ringing of a bell.

Early the next morning Bishop Hieronymo sang the mass and absolved all the Christians from their sins; praying afterwards, warlike man that he was, to be the first to drive back the enemy. Whilst it was still dark, the Cid, well armed and mounted on Bavieca, went out with his company at the gate which was called the Gate of the Snake. They loitered about at first, and then when the Cid rang his bell the Christians came out of their hiding-places amongst the narrow ways and passes, and the Moors were shut in between their enemies and the sea. There was hard fighting that day; the Moors, arming themselves in haste, made a firm stand, but before night they were overcome and fled to Denia, leaving great riches behind them in the camp. Ruy Diaz, who had been wounded in the battle, rode joyfully back to the city when they were gone, still mounted on Bavieca, and with his drawn sword still in his hand; and he sent King Alonzo a present of three hundred horses laden with the gold and silver he had found amongst the spoils.

Yusef died soon after his defeat, and his brother Bucar swore upon the Koran, the book of their law, that he would take revenge upon the mighty Castillian chief.

The Infantes of Carrion, Diego, and Fernan Gonzalez, vassals of King Alonzo in Castille, having heard how the power of the Cid was increasing day by day, demanded his daughters in marriage, thinking by so doing they would become rich and powerful themselves. The Cid was pleased with the proposal, but Doña Ximena did not like the idea of such a marriage at all; however, since the king had heartily approved of it, she dared say nothing against it.

The weddings were performed by Bishop Hieronymo, and there were great rejoicings in Valencia for eight days. Each day had its festival, either in bull-fighting, or tilting, or shooting stones from the cross-bow, or they witnessed the performances of the Moorish jugglers and buffoons, who were very clever in their art. Then there were magnificent banquets in the Alcazar, the tables being covered with silver dishes filled with rare and highly-seasoned meats.

For two years the Infantes lived with their wives at Valencia in peace; but at the end of that time a misfortune happened, which caused them to break with their father-in-law, although it was no fault of his. The Cid had a very large and lively lion, which afforded him great amusement, and was kept in an iron house, which opened into a high court behind the Alcazar; three men had the charge of it, and it was their custom about mid-day to open the door of its house, and let it come into the court to eat its dinner, taking care before they left to fasten the door of the court securely.

The Cid used to dine in company every day, and after dinner he sometimes fell asleep, for he was getting old. One day a man came to him, and told him that many vessels had arrived before Valencia, having on board a great host of the Moors, and among them Bucar, the African king, who had sworn to revenge the death of his brother. When the Cid heard this he was very much pleased, for it was nearly three years since he had had a fight with the Moors. He had his bell rung as a sign that all the honourable men in the city should assemble, and when they came to Alcazar, and the Infantes were there too, he told them the news, and agreed with them as to the manner in which they should repel the advance of their foes. When this was done he went quietly to sleep, and Diego and Fernan, and the rest of the company sat playing at tables [9] and at chess.

It happened that the men who guarded the lion heard that the Moors had come, and rushed to the palace to see if the news were true, forgetting in their anxiety to close the door of the court behind them. And lo and behold! the lion, when it had dined right royally, and saw the door open, walked out of the court and straight into the great hall where all the company were assembled. It certainly was an alarming sight, and the people did not know what to do, fearing that the lion might be roused to fury and tear some of them to pieces. Diego and Fernan Gonzalez showed more terror and cowardice than all the rest, and Diego ran and hid himself under the Cid's chair, and very nearly died of fright in his undignified retreat, whilst Fernan rushed out of a gallery which led into a court where there was a winepress, and entering therein he tumbled among the lees, which served him quite right.

The others remained in the hall, and stood around the Cid to guard him while he slept. The noise of their talking, however, at last awakened him, and he saw how the lion came towards him and licked his hand, and he asked what it meant. And when the lion heard his voice, it stood quite quiet, and the Cid arose and took it by the neck as if it had been a hound, and made it go back to its iron house, calmly giving orders that it should be more strictly guarded in future.

When the Infantes came out of their hiding-places they must have felt very much ashamed, but they gave a very different version of the story to what had really happened. In the famous poem of the Cid, which contains a great deal of historic truth, Ruy Diaz forbears reproaching his sons-in-law for their cowardice. Be that as it may, they made the event a pretence for taking offence with him, as they were wicked and discontented men; they were tired of their wives, and thought that they ought to have wedded damsels of far higher rank than the daughters of the Cid. So they said that he had arranged that the lion should come out of its den only to put them to shame before all the hidalgos; and their uncle, Suero Gonzalez, wickedly advised them to ask Ruy Diaz to let them take their wives to their home in Carrion, that, once out of Valencia, they might do with them whatsoever they pleased.

In the meantime there was much noise in the city. Bucar had landed his forces, and arrived in a plain about a league from Valencia, which was called Quarto; and there the Cid gave him such a defeat that he was obliged to flee with his diminished army across the sea. Ruy Diaz was still kindly disposed towards his sons-in-law; and when the battle was over he thanked them for the share they had had in it, when they had really done nothing at all, and had only pretended to fight; such men were not worthy to have married the daughters of the Cid! Now they said that they had heard no news of their father and mother in Carrion since they left Castille; and they wanted to take their wives home, and tell their parents what honour they had attained to by marrying them. Doña Ximena had no faith in them, and she told her husband that they were not true-hearted; she was very loth to let her daughters go with them; nevertheless the Cid trusted them still, and one day Elvira and Sol set out from Valencia with the Infantes; their parents, and a great and valiant company going with them two leagues on the road to Castille. Before they started, Ruy Diaz gave them presents worthy of a king. First of all, he gave them a quantity of cloth of gold, silk, and wool, a hundred horses richly caparisoned, and a hundred mules with gorgeous trappings; then he gave them ten goblets of pure gold, and a hundred vases of silver besides quantities of silver in plate and shields. A hundred well-appointed knights were to accompany them into Castille; amongst whom were two very brave men, named Martin Pelaez and Pero Sanchez, whom the Cid held in great esteem. Last of all he gave the Infantes each a golden-hilted sword to defend their wives with; these two swords he prized very much, because he had won them from the Moors, and he had named them Colada and Tizona.

When it was time to part, Elvira and Sol took a sorrowful leave of their parents, and the Cid, as he turned away from them began to feel some misgivings in his heart, and to wonder if Ximena had really been right in her distrust. The Infantes, however, still promised to treat their wives with honour, and the cavalcade went on towards Castille. On the way they were entertained by a Moorish king, a vassal of the Cid's, who could not do enough to show his pleasure in welcoming them, and so far all was well, and they went through the valleys until they reached the oak forest of Torpes. When they arrived there the Infantes told all the knights to go forward, and said they would stay for a while in the forest. Elvira asked her husband Diego why they remained there alone; he replied that she should soon see. Then these wicked men took their wives by the hair and dragged them along until they came to the fountain of Torpes, and there they beat them with the leathern girths of their saddles until the blood flowed from their wounds. And they took from them all the costly jewels, and robes of silk and ermine Doña Ximena had given them, and went on their way, leaving the poor ladies half dead by themselves in the forest, where the wild beasts might have come and devoured them. Elvira and Sol startled the birds in the branches overhead by the piteous cries they uttered in their terror and pain; then, finding that no one came to their aid, they said their prayers very fervently, and sank fainting to the ground.

The cruel Infantes mounted their horses, and took the mules which had carried their wives, and said aloud as they went out of the forest, "Now we have done with the daughters of the Cid! We demeaned ourselves by marrying them, and we are avenged of the affront their father put upon us by letting loose the lion."

Felez Nuñoz, however, the nephew of the Cid, happened to pass that way, and he heard what the Infantes said. He would have punished them on the spot, but he feared they would return and perhaps kill their wives; so he went into the deep oak glades, and kept calling his cousins by their names until he found them. Then, in great sorrow to behold the terrible plight they were in, he gave them water to drink, and carried them to a part of the forest where they would be in greater safety, and made a soft couch for them of tender green leaves and grass, whereon they might rest, for they were utterly worn out.

The knights had gone on their way, and when they saw the Infantes coming towards them bringing with them the mules and the rich robes of their wives, they began to fear that some evil deed had been done, and they all crowded round them, taunting them with their cowardice, and threatening to fight them. The Infantes wanted to be rid of them all, and declared that if the knights would go back to the forest, they would find Elvira and Sol by the fountain there unharmed. So Martin Pelaez and Pero Sanchez, and all the bravest men in the company returned thither; but when Felez Nuñoz and his cousins heard their voices they were alarmed, thinking the Infantes were near; and they kept quite still, so that the knights could not find them, and returned, very angry, to pursue the cowardly brothers, feeling sure that some foul deed had been done. Diego and Fernan, however, were already beyond their pursuit,—craven-hearted men can fly fast, and the knights set out at once for the court of Don Alonzo, and told their king all that had happened.

Now the ladies in the forest at first had nothing to eat, and were very near dying of hunger, when, by good fortune Felez Nuñoz found his way to a village where he bought them food, and he kept them thus from starving for seven days; but could not make their misfortunes known to the Cid because he feared to leave them by themselves in the wild forest. At last he found in his village a worthy man in whose house the Cid had once lodged, and he brought two asses to the forest, and made the noble ladies mount them, and led them in safety to his own house, where his wife tended them kindly, rejoicing that she had them under her roof. Here they wrote a letter to their father, which Felez Nuñoz undertook to convey to him at Valencia. On the road thither he met Alvar Fanez and Pero Bermudez, who were going to the king with a present from Ruy Diaz, of two hundred horses he had won in his battle with Bucar, besides a number of swords and a hundred Moorish captives. These knights were enabled to give Don Alonzo a faithful account of all that had happened, and the king was very indignant at the wickedness of his vassals, and appointed a day, three months from the time, when he would hear the matter through, and give judgment in his Cortes at Toledo. And Alvar and Pero set out in search of the Cid's daughters, taking with them from Alonzo two mules, with saddles richly adorned with gold, and jewelled robes for the sisters, so that they might return to Valencia in the same attire they had worn when they started on their hapless journey. When they had found them at the good man's house, Pero went on to Valencia, and Alvar remained with the knights who had followed him to guard his cousins. The indignation and anger of the mighty Cid may be imagined when he heard how his children had been treated.

Doña Ximena was more dead than alive, and she was thankful indeed when she had her dear daughters safe at home with her once more.

Great preparations were made for the day of trial. The walls of the palace, where judgment was to be given, were hung with cloth of gold, rich carpets were spread on the floor, and a great throne was placed in readiness for the king. The Cid left Hieronymo and Martin Pelaez in charge of his city, and set out betimes for Toledo with so great a host of followers that it looked like an army. When he drew near Alonzo came out to meet him, but he would not cross the Tagus that night, and had candles lighted in the church of Saint Servans on the shore, and kept a vigil there a great part of the night with his friends. And he ordered one of his hidalgos to set a beautiful ivory chair he had won from the Moors close beside the king's throne, and sent a hundred squires, each one an hidalgo, to stand around it all night to guard it, with swords hanging from their necks.

There were many people in Toledo who were friends of the Infantes of Carrion, and therefore ill-disposed towards the Cid, and they thought he was taking a great liberty in having his chair set beside the king's throne: but Alonzo honoured him, and he suffered it to remain.

It was a stately meeting; we are told that when the day came Ruy Diaz wore a tunic of gold tissue, and over that a red skin with points of gold; this he always wore, and on his head he had a coif of scarlet and gold: his long beard, which was getting white, was tied up with a cord. [10] When he came into the hall, the king and all the people stood up, except those who were on the side of the Infantes of Carrion.

Alonzo gave judgment against those wicked men, and made them give up the golden-hilted swords Colada and Tizona, which they did not indeed deserve to keep. But the Cid was not content when judgment was pronounced; he thought the dishonour was not yet wiped away, and he stood up and required that three knights should fight for his cause against three of Carrion.

When he said this the three brave knights named Martin Antolinez, Pero Bermudez, and Nuno Gustios, entreated him to let them fight on his side; and a terrible quarrel arose; the Infantes said many rude things of the Cid, and his haughty hidalgos would not suffer their insults to pass; they quarrelled and fought until the king could scarcely hear himself speak, and he rose from his seat and called the Alcaydes, and went to confer with them in a chamber apart, while the Cid and all the others remained in the hall. When he came back he sat down on his throne with great solemnity, and told the people to listen to the sentence, which decreed that a combat should take place three weeks from that day between the Infantes and their uncle

Suero Gonzalez on the side of Carrion, and the three brave knights who were willing to fight for the Cid.

Ruy Diaz was now content; he rose from his seat and kissed the king's hand, and prayed that God might have him in His holy keeping for many good years, so that he might administer justice worthily, as he had done that day.

In the midst of all this, messengers arrived at the palace from the kings of Arragon and Navarre, demanding the daughters of the Cid in marriage for their sons, when the unhappy marriage they had made with the Infantes of Carrion should be dissolved. Ruy Diaz went back to Valencia in joy, and told the glad news to his wife; adding that they need have no fear now for their daughters' happiness, because the princes of Arragon and Navarre were known far and wide to be honourable men. The combat took place on the appointed day. The Cid lent Colada and Tizona to his knights, and Diego and Fernan Gonzalez, and their uncle Suero, were all three overcome and wounded in the presence of King Alonzo; and, they crept away in disgrace and were never seen more, and Carrion, after the death of Don Gonzalez, their father, went back to the crown of Castille.

When the three victorious knights returned safe and sound to Valencia, and made known there the result of the combat, the joy of the Cid was beyond all bounds, and as for Doña Ximena, and Elvira, and Sol, they would fain have kissed the feet of their valiant defenders. There was rejoicing in the city for eight days, and banquets were held every day, the silver dishes being filled with the flesh of many extraordinary animals, which were cooked in Spain for the first time, having been sent to the Cid with a number of rare and beautiful presents from the Soldan, or Sultan of Persia. The Soldan paid great court to Ruy Diaz, and made known to him how a vast army of Christians had come out to the East and lay before Jerusalem, hoping to conquer that city from the Saracens; and that was the first crusade which had been preached by Peter the Hermit, when William Rufus was reigning in England.

The Cid remained in peace at Valencia for five years, and kept the Moors so quiet that they no longer molested the Christians, but lived with them on friendly terms. At the end of this time news came suddenly that Bucar had stirred up all the chiefs in Barbary to cross the sea in revenge for the victory that Ruy Diaz had gained over him in the field of Quarto.

The Cid sent the Moors who dwelt in the city to the suburb of Alcudia, where he thought they had better remain until the affair was ended. His strength was failing fast; and one night, as he lay wakeful on his bed, his chamber was filled with a strange brightness and fragrance, and he had another wonderful vision, in which Saint Peter appeared to him, aged and white as snow, with a bunch of keys in his hand, and told him now to mind other things besides the coming of Bucar, for that in thirty days he should die, and yet by the help of Saint James he should conquer his foes after he was dead. When the vision disappeared the Cid was lost in wonder, but he felt greatly comforted; and early in the morning he called the hidalgos around him and told them what he had seen, and how they should conquer the Moors. The last day that he was able to rise from his bed he ordered the city gates to be shut, and repaired to the church of Saint Peter, where he spoke long and earnestly to the people assembled there, reminding them that, however great and honourable their estate in life might be, not one of them could escape death. Then he took leave of them all, and confessed his sins at the feet of Bishop Hieronymo. From that time until his death, seven days afterwards, he took no nourishment except a little myrrh and balsam stirred in rose water, such as was used to embalm the dead bodies of kings in the East, and had been sent among the gifts of the Soldan in a casket of gold. He bequeathed great riches to his knights, leaving a thousand marks of silver to those who had only served him one year, and he ordered four thousand poor persons to be clothed at his expense. On Sunday, the 25th of May, 1099, the Cid died, in the seventy-third year of his age. These were his dying words: "Lord Jesus Christ, Thine is the kingdom; Thou art above all kings and all nations, and all kings are at Thy command. I beseech Thee to pardon my sins, and let my soul enter the light that hath no end."

Three days after his death King Bucar came, and with him thirty-six kings or chiefs. It is said that fifteen thousand tents were pitched around Valencia. As all was quiet inside the city, the Africans thought that their enemy dared not come out against them.

Meanwhile the body of the Cid had been embalmed and fixed in a wooden frame upright upon Bavieca, and the frame being painted to represent armour, it looked really as if he were alive. A mournful procession went out at midnight from the gate towards Castille. First the banner of the Cid was carried, guarded by five hundred knights; then came one hundred more, around the body of their lord; and lastly, Ximena followed sorrowfully with all her company, and three hundred knights in the rear. By the time they had all passed out the summer night was spent, and it was broad daylight.

Alvar Funez now fell upon the Moors with the forces that remained in Valencia; and so great was the terror and uproar he caused that they fled towards the sea, leaving their riches for the spoils of the Christians. The Moors who had retired to the suburb saw the procession pass, and thought that their lord had gone forth alive. But when they entered the city from whence all the Spanish knights had gone, they marvelled at the strange silence in the streets, until they saw written on the walls in Arabic that the Cid Campeador was dead. From that day Valencia remained in the power of the Moors until it was won by King Jayme of Arragon, in the year 1238; but the city was always known by the name of "Valencia of the Cid."

The body of Ruy Diaz was placed in his ivory chair at the right of the altar of Saint Peter in the church of Cardeña. It was clothed in purple cloth which had been given to him by the Soldan, and remained thus more than ten years. When that time had passed it was buried in a vault beside the grave of Doña Ximena, who only survived him three years. And Bavieca, his favourite horse, was buried not far from his master, under some trees in front of the convent of Saint Peter of Cardeña.

FOOTNOTES:

[7] Like the Alhambra court in the Crystal Palace.

[8] *Sol*, Spanish for sun.

[9] *Tablas*, in the Spanish tables, probably the game of draughts.

[10] See Southey's "Chronicle."

LOUIS IX.
KING OF FRANCE

The good king Louis the Ninth, commonly called St. Louis, because he led so holy a life, was born at Poissy, in the year 1215, whilst his grandfather, Philip Augustus, was still on the throne of France. Poissy was a beautiful place, just as Fontainebleau is now, where the kings of France used to go and hunt, and enjoy the sweet fresh air; and the queens passed many happy days with their little children, away from the cares and the splendour of the court.

Louis was always of a meek and gentle disposition, truthful and upright. His mother, Blanche of Castille, watched over him tenderly herself, and took care to place around him as early as possible the holiest and most learned men in France, in the hope that through their influence he might grow up to be a good king. Blanche was a woman of great piety, and she was very clever and beautiful besides; she had many children, but although Louis was always her favourite amongst them all, she did not indulge him either in luxury or pleasure, and used often to say to him, "My son, I love you more than I can tell; yet I would rather see you lying dead at my feet than know you were guilty of a mortal sin."

Louis did indeed try earnestly to be good, and to remember the words of his mother; he was obedient to his instructors, and is said to have understood Latin well, and to have been versed in the works of the fathers of the Church, and in the history of the kings who reigned before him; and that was knowing a great deal, for the times he lived in were called "the dark ages," because so very little was learnt or known, especially in Europe. His amusements were hunting and fishing, and playing at chess, but he did not care for these as he cared for the services of the church, attending them daily with his little brothers, and loving the holy chants and hymns he heard there more than any songs of merriment.

Louis was only eleven years old when his father, King Louis the Eighth, died, after a reign of less than four years. He had then four brothers younger than himself—Robert, John, Alphonse, and Charles; and one little sister named Isabel. As he was so very young, his mother, Queen Blanche, governed his kingdom for him, and she had many troubles to contend with, on account of the quarrels and revolts of some of the most powerful nobles in the land. Several of these refused to attend the coronation of Louis, which took place at Rheims, after he had been knighted, according to the custom of the time, at Soissons. The ceremony was very solemn; Queen Blanche would not let it be made an occasion of rejoicing, because her heart was so full of sorrow for the death of her husband; and the day after she took Louis to Paris, and began at once to think what would be the best measures for securing his safety and the welfare of the country.

It was at the siege of Bellesme that Louis gained his first experience in war, when he was only twelve years of age. The Count de Bretagne, foremost of the rebellious nobles, had invaded the territory of the king, and was causing great misery to the country people by laying waste their land and destroying their villages. To chastise him, and bring him to obedience, Queen Blanche set off in the depth of winter with her son Louis and only a few followers, to lay siege to the Castle of Bellesme, where the count had first set up his standard of rebellion.

The snow lay deep on the ground, and icicles hung from the trees along the road-side: the cold was intense, and the march was difficult in the short winter days, but little Louis was as brave as he was gentle, and cared nothing for the cold and discomfort, nor did he tremble the least at the idea of the coming affray; his mother had taught him to endure manfully hardships and pain and fatigue, and to trust in God, whatever danger was at hand.

The Castle of Bellesme exists no longer; its ruins have long crumbled away: in those days it was a strong fortress, surrounded by thick walls flanked with towers. The Count of Bretagne was inside the castle with all the bravest of his men, and the queen's party made two assaults upon it in vain. The cold had numbed the energies of the knights and the soldiers in the camp, and they were very nearly frozen to death. Queen Blanche then published a decree which promised large rewards to all persons who should cut down the trees in the forests around, and bring the wood to the camp. The peasants were soon seen joyfully bringing the wood on their shoulders and in carts: enormous fires were kindled, and the warmth so quickly restored the spirits of the besiegers, that before two days had passed, the greater part of the fortification was thrown down, and the haughty Count de Bretagne, seeing no hope of succour, was obliged to surrender. Queen Blanche and her little son treated the garrison with great kindness when they came out; and a treaty was soon after made, by which it was agreed that Louis's brother John should marry, when he grew up, the daughter of the Count de Bretagne.

Whilst Louis was growing out of childhood, and striving day by day to become more holy in the sight of God, the rebellions of the nobles were continually breaking out afresh, and had to be put down by force of arms, or the crown would have lost much of its power. This chapter, however, is not to be a record of all the disturbances that occurred in France during the early part of the good king's reign, but rather a description of the events which brought to light most strikingly his piety, his courage, and his patience.

In the year 1233 Louis was persuaded by his mother to bestow his hand on Marguerite, daughter of Raymond Berenger, Count of Provence. Raymond had four daughters, and Marguerite was the most beautiful and talented of them all. Her sister Eleanor was married soon after to Henry the Third of England, and another sister, named Beatrice, to Louis's brother Charles, Count of Anjou.

The royal marriage was celebrated with great magnificence at Sens; and when Louis was twenty years of age he took the reins of government into his own hands: nevertheless Queen Blanche continued to influence him by her advice, and was obeyed by him until her death, on all occasions save one, as will be seen hereafter.

The peace of the country was not really established until the year 1239, when some of the quarrelsome nobles had gone on a crusade to the Holy Land. The enterprise did not succeed; the Christian army was entrapped and defeated by the Saracens, and Jerusalem became a possession of the Sultan of Egypt. The king was deeply grieved at the failure; he was always thinking of the miseries and oppressions the Christians were forced to endure in the East, and resolved to go and help them as soon as he could leave his country in prosperity. When the rumour of this was spread in Palestine, the sheik, or old man of the mountain, singled out the King of France for his victim, and despatched two of his assassins to Paris, thinking thus to put an end to all idea of a fresh crusade.

Having boasted, however, of his intended deed before some of the knights templars, he was told by them that if he put Louis to death, his brothers would certainly avenge the crime, and draw upon him the ill will of many nations besides France. The sheik now became as anxious to preserve the king's life as he had been to take it, and sent off in a great hurry two of his emirs to the court of France to warn Louis of his danger. The king received the intelligence calmly, and only instituted another company of guards, who were armed with maces of brass. But when the assassins could not be discovered, notwithstanding the marks by which the emirs declared they would be known, these men hastened to Marseilles, and luckily arrived there before the Arabs set foot on shore. When they had told them how the sheik had determined not to take the king's life, they conducted them to Paris, and all four were received with kindness by Louis, and went back to the East much impressed with the magnificence of the French court; for although the king loved neither luxury nor pleasure, his court was always kept up with dignity and splendour. The Sire de Joinville, who was twenty-two years in his company, tells us how, at a great festival held at Saumur, which was called a plenary court, the king wore a coat of blue samite, a species of satin, with overcoat and mantle of crimson samite, bordered with ermine, and strangely enough, a cotton cap on his head, which did not become him at all. His hair, which was fair, he wore short, according to the custom of the time. At this feast there were at least three thousand knights present, and so many robes of cloth of gold and of silk had never been seen before. King Louis, his brothers, and the King of Navarre sat at one table, Joinville himself carving for them; the queen mother and her ladies sat at another, and the archbishops and bishops at a third; and to guard the king's table stood three of the greatest barons in the land; and to guard them stood thirty knights, in garments of rich silken stuff; and these again had a retinue of the royal officers behind them.

During the whole time that the plenary courts were held, the king was obliged to dine in public, and it was an old custom, that before the dinner was ended, three heralds at arms, each with a rich cap in his hand, cried out three times, "Bounty of the most powerful King!" and then threw gold and silver to the people, so that the poor had their share of the rejoicing as well as the rich.

The king was seized with a dangerous illness at Pontoise in the year 1244. This was a very great sorrow for his people, since it was feared that he would die, and they joined in solemn processions all over the kingdom, and went to the churches to pray to the Almighty to restore him to health. Queen Blanche was the saddest of all, and passed her time between the sick chamber of her son, and the foot of the altar, where she knelt for hours in silent prayer.

When Louis felt that he was getting weaker, he sent for all the members of his household, and thanked them for their services; after which he recommended them to serve God with earnest and faithful hearts. Then he sank into a lethargy, which those who were watching by his bedside at first mistook for death. The lethargy lasted several days, and then the king gave signs of returning life. The first words he spoke after opening his eyes were these:—"By the grace of God the light of the East has shone upon me from the height of heaven, and recalled me from the dead." He summoned the Bishop of Paris to his presence, and required him to affix the cross to his shoulder, as a sign that he bound himself to go on the crusade.

The sorrow which had been forgotten when the king gave signs of recovery, now broke out afresh. The two queens, Blanche and Marguerite, threw themselves on their knees, and implored him with many tears not to go on the crusade; even the bishops, who stood by, tried to persuade him not to engage in so difficult an enterprise, but all in vain. Louis would take no nourishment until the cross was really fastened to his shoulder; and his people heard of the vow he had taken in gloom and regret, for they thought if he once set sail for the Holy Land, they would never see him again.

The king did not really recover until several months had passed, and then he wrote to the Christians in the East to tell them that he was coming to their aid. But it was a long time yet before he was able to set out, because he loved his people very dearly, and wanted to provide everything for their comfort and happiness during his absence, when his mother, Queen Blanche, was to rule over them in his stead. He persuaded the most turbulent of the nobles to go with him on the crusade, and when the best measures had been taken for securing the peace of the kingdom, he made known that he was ready to redress every injury he had offered, it being the custom then for all good crusaders to make their peace with God and man before they embarked in their enterprise.

Louis then went with his brothers, Robert of Artois and Charles of Anjou, to the church of Saint Denis to receive his pilgrim's scrip and staff, and the oriflamme, or sacred banner of Saint Denis. This was a banner of flame-coloured silk, which was always carried before the French armies on solemn occasions for the encouragement of the soldiers. The king, having requested all holy persons to pray that his undertaking might prove successful, came back to Paris, and heard mass at the great church of Notre Dame, and then went out of the city he was not to behold again for so long, followed by the clergy, the nobles, and multitudes of the common people.

The crimson and the samite, the gold-embroidered garments with the ermines, were now laid aside for a plain grey robe trimmed with grey and white fur. The trappings of the king's horses were no longer adorned with gold, but the steel of their harness was polished until it shone like silver. Louis computed before he left France how much his former luxuries had cost him yearly, and then caused the amount to be regularly distributed to the poor.

At Cluny, Queen Blanche bade her son a long sad farewell: it was the first time he had ever thwarted her wishes by refusing to give up the crusade, when she urged that a vow made in a time of extreme weakness was not binding. His young wife could not bring herself to part with him, and declared she would follow him to the end of the world.

When all was ready, the king, with his brothers Robert and Charles, Queen Marguerite, and the young Countess of Anjou, and a vast number of crusaders of all nations, embarked at Aigues-Mortes, a port on the Mediterranean, which had been constructed for the occasion. They took the direction of Cyprus, and the winds being favourable, all the vessels except one, which was unhappily shipwrecked, reached the island in safety. Here the crusaders remained during the winter. For two years before they arrived, the king's people had been bringing wine and various provisions for the army from the most fertile countries of Europe, and had laid up their store in the island. The tubs of wine they had piled one upon the other, until they looked like great barns; and the wheat and the barley lay in heaps in the fields, green on the outside, where the warm rains falling softly upon them had made them sprout. The crusaders found an abundant supply of food in Cyprus, without having recourse to their stores, and when in the spring they wanted to set out for Egypt, they took off the outer covering of the heaps, and saw the wheat and the barley beneath, as fresh as if it had just been cut.

The departure from the island was fixed for Ascension Day in the year 1249. The crusaders embarked towards evening at the port called Limesson, where they had landed. The vessels large and small amounted to 1,650, and were thronged with a vast assembly of people of all callings and nations, 2,800 of them being knights. The next day the king sent a sealed packet into every vessel, with orders for it to remain unopened until the fleet had set sail; the purport of this was that they should proceed direct to Damietta. The wind, however, blew against them, and forced them to return to the port; and when they had got out to sea again a few days after, a violent tempest arose from the side of Egypt, and scattered all the vessels. Louis himself was obliged to go back to the port of Limesson, and found on arriving there that his fleet was diminished by one hundred and twenty vessels, and that the number of knights was reduced to seven hundred! But he would not suffer the followers who remained to him to be cast down, and on Trinity Sunday they set sail once more, and although in continual dread of another storm, they went on their way safely, until a sailor who knew the coasts of Egypt, and served as a guide, warned them that they were before Damietta, the great stronghold of the Saracens in Egypt. All the other vessels now crowded around the one which bore the king, who stood up among his people calm and trustful, encouraging them to persevere for the love of God, and not to flinch in the moment of danger.

Saleh, the Sultan, was at some distance from Damietta; he was supposed to be dying, and had confided the care of his army to the emir Facardin. The Saracens had seen the sea covered with masts and sails by seven o'clock in the morning, and had rung the bell of their great mosque to spread the alarm in the city: the Christians heard the sound across the sea in the clear summer air. Facardin ordered four Corsair vessels to approach the fleet, but three of these ventured too near, and were overwhelmed by showers of stones from the larger vessels. The fourth went back to convey the tidings that the King of France had come with a number of foreign princes.

At mid-day the fleet of the Christians cast anchor in the roads of Damietta. The port was full of men-of-war, and the flat country of Egypt was covered with rich tents, whilst crowds of people on foot and on horse stood along the shore, sounding their twisted horns, and their great cymbals, two of which were a sufficient load for an elephant; and making, as the Sire de Joinville affirms, "a sound horrible to be heard!"

A council was held on board the king's vessel, at which it was resolved to land the next day, although only a portion of the fleet had as yet arrived in the roads; but Louis thought that delay would inspire fear, and perhaps afford the Saracens the opportunity of destroying his army by degrees. So when it got dark, the crusaders lighted a great number of torches, and kept watch all night; and they confessed their sins one to another, and prayed for those they loved, and had left behind in Europe; and as many as had quarrelled made friends, that they might be ready for death, if it should meet them in the struggle on the morrow.

At daybreak they lifted anchor, and sailed for the island of Giza, which was joined to Damietta by a bridge of boats across the river Nile. The king commanded his people to get down into the flat boats they had brought with them, because the large vessels could not approach the shore: the boat Joinville was in soon distanced the one which bore the Oriflamme, and was first to gain the land.

Suddenly the air was darkened by a flight of arrows from the bows of the Saracens. Louis, seeing this, gave orders for each man to disembark as he could, and jumped from his boat into the water, covered as he was by his armour, with his shield on his breast, and his sword in his hand. The water was deeper there than elsewhere, and he was immersed up to his shoulders, but the sight of the Oriflamme safely landed encouraged him in his efforts, and he got to the shore before any of the others. Although countless swords and pike points were aimed at him as he landed, the good king did not forget to kneel down for a moment on the sand, to thank the Almighty for having preserved him thus far; then, rising, he would have rushed on the Saracens at once and alone, if his knights, who were now gaining their footing on shore, had not prevented him.

All the rest now followed; Louis put his people in battle array as they landed, and ordered an attack to be made on some of the enemy's larger vessels. Before the day was ended the Christian army had driven the Saracens from the western shores of the Nile, and had got possession of the bridge of boats; they would have pursued their foes, but night coming on, the king sounded a retreat, and encamped on the ground he had conquered. Meanwhile the poor queen and the Countess of Anjou had been in terrible anxiety and distress when they watched from their vessel afar the multitudes rushing into the water, and could not tell whether their husbands were alive or drowned. And great must have been their joy when the news was conveyed to him that those they loved so dearly were safe on shore, and that their efforts, as yet, had been crowned with success.

Early the next morning, which was Sunday, the king was giving orders for the siege of Damietta, when two Christian captives came to the camp and told him that the city was deserted. The king could scarcely credit their words, and sent one of his knights to the spot to see if they were really true. The knight returned with the same account; the Saracens had gone back to Damietta in great distress the evening before, and on their arrival had heard that the Sultan was dead.

The rumour struck dismay into the heart of Facardin, and he only waited to put the Christian slaves who were in the city to death, and to burn the bazaars where the provisions were sold, and then he went out at the gates the same night with his army and the garrison; old men and women, children and sick persons following in the rear of the craven-hearted troops, until by daylight the whole city was deserted.

Damietta was now open to the Christians; they had only to cross the bridge of boats and enter its gates. The king in his thankfulness thought that he ought not to enter the city as a triumphant warrior, but humbly, and clad as a pilgrim; and he walked thither barefoot, followed by the King of Cyprus, who had joined the crusade, the patriarch of Jerusalem, the legate, and all the bishops and priests who had accompanied the army. A mosque, where the Saracens had worshipped, was hastily converted into a Christian church, and a solemn chant of thanksgiving ascended from its altar. The crusaders had indeed reason to be thankful because Damietta was so strong a place, protected by a double wall on the side of the Nile, and by a triple one on the side of the flat country. The king determined to remain there until the autumn, and thus avoid marching in the great heat, and the danger which his army would be exposed to from the rising of the Nile, for the river begins to rise in the month of June, and mounts higher and higher until September, overflowing the land along its course so that it looks like a great marsh, and the villages and trees appear like islands above the water.

By November the fields are dry again and covered with a rich brown slime, and the people then begin to sow their corn. The soil being so fertile, in the winter months the valley of the Nile presents the appearance of a beautiful garden; indeed, the natives are obliged sometimes to mix sand with the loam, or the fruits and vegetables would grow and ripen too quickly.

When the water had risen to a certain height, the Saracens used to open their dykes with great solemnity and let it flow over the land; and it was remembered with sadness in the Christian camp how they had used it for the destruction of the crusading army in the enterprise which had failed only a few years before.

The queen and her sister, with their ladies in attendance, were lodged in one of the palaces in the city, and the pilgrims who had come in the hope of reaching Jerusalem in another; but the king remained in his tent outside with the army.

The crusaders soon began to suffer from the intense heat of the climate, and the flies and noxious insects which infested the camp.

The report of the sultan's death had been false. Saleh was still living, but almost at his last gasp; and finding he could not dictate to the King of France the hour when a battle should take place between them, he devised a sure method of annoyance by offering a reward of a besant of gold for every head of a Christian which should be brought to him. The Arabs or Bedouins undertook to perform this service. Clad only in the skins of wild beasts, they would suddenly appear in the camp, and vanish on their swift-footed horses as soon as they were seen. On dark nights they used to put their ear to the ground, as the Arabs do to this day, and listen if the night watch had gone its rounds before they began their dread work; and as there were always people sleeping on the outskirts of the camp, who had gone out in search of prey, scarcely a night passed but some heads were missing at daybreak. The king, to mislead them, ordered the night watch to be made by foot soldiers instead of horsemen, but it did not prevent the maurauders from coming, and at last the crusaders had to dig a deep trench all round the camp as a surer means of keeping them away.

Louis was anxiously awaiting the arrival of his brother Alphonse, Count of Poitou, Prince John being left in France to assist the queen-mother in the cares of the government. The Count came at last, bringing with him the wife of Robert of Artois. The time was wearing on, and a council was held to determine which way they should next proceed. Robert, who was as zealous in the crusade as Louis himself, but who had not his brother's patience and calmness of mind, strongly advised that they should pursue the road to Cairo, or Babylon, as it was then called, and so aim a blow at the whole dominion of the Sultan in Egypt. The king yielded to his wishes, and leaving the queen and the princesses in the city, with a sufficient number of guards to protect them, he set out from Damietta, although he was in weak health from the effects of the climate. The army crossed the bridge of boats, but it could only go slowly along; there were so many things, such as engines, arms, harness, and provisions, to be transported. The crusaders imagined that they were going to Babylon, the great city of the East, on the banks of the Euphrates; but the city they were approaching was only so named by some settlers from the Eastern Babylon, and was what is now called "Old Cairo," although in those days it was almost as great a place as Memphis, the ancient capital of Egypt. They were much astonished at the abundant vegetation on the shores of the Nile, and the treasures to be found even in its waters; for the Sire de Joinville tells us how the country people used to throw their nets into the river at evening, and take them up in the morning filled with cinnamon, aloes, ginger, rhubarb, and things of a like nature; the common belief being that these riches dropped from the trees in the garden of paradise, and were wafted up the river to their feet!

The Egyptian fleet was stationed at Massoura, a city nearly a third of the way between Damietta and Cairo. The sultan was now dead, but his widow would not let it be known until her son could arrive to take the government into his hands, for fear that the people should get discouraged.

The crusaders had not gone far from Damietta, when they found their passage barred by the Thanis, a branch of the Nile, the opposite shore of which was guarded by a body of five hundred Saracen horsemen. The Thanis was the river they had to cross; it was deep near its steep shores; there was no bridge, neither did they know of a ford, so they encamped on the ground which formed the extremity of the angle between the two rivers, only separated from the town of Massourah by the stream and a part of the plain. Their situation soon became very dangerous, because the Saracens were constantly attacking their side which was unprotected by the waters: the machines of the enemy, too, were better than their own, and poured upon them a continual volley of stones, darts, javelins, arrows, and heavy pieces of wood. Then at night the Saracens would throw upon them their terrible Greek fire, which appeared with a loud hissing noise, "like a fiery dragon flying through the air," and rendered the camp as light as day. The Saracens were more skilful in the art of making fireworks than the Europeans, and always employed them in warfare. The basis of the Greek fire was naphtha, a clear, thin mineral fluid, which is very inflammable, and burns with much smoke. When it came, the Christians would throw themselves down on the ground and hide their faces, and the king, whenever he heard it explode in the night, would rise in his bed and say, "Blessed Lord God, save my people!" and every night he would send round the camp to inquire who had been injured by it. Sometimes it was put out with vinegar and sand, but it usually occasioned great harm, not only to the people in the camp, but also to the machines.

The king, having tried in vain to construct a dyke, had now to think seriously of returning to Damietta, or of remaining in this corner between the rivers, surrounded by the enemy, and almost in total want of provisions. He was about to retreat, notwithstanding the sorrow and disappointment it cost him to give up the enterprise, when a Bedouin, who had abandoned the Saracens, came to the camp and said that he knew of a ford which the horsemen might pass, and would show it to them for the sum of five hundred besants of gold, but not until he had the money safe in his hand.

The king joyfully accepted his offer, and arranged that the Duke of Burgundy should be left with the infantry to guard the camp, whilst he, with his brothers and all the rest, should attempt the passage. The Count of Artois begged for the honour of passing first, and the king somewhat reluctantly granted him his request, on condition that he should not venture to fight until the whole army had assembled; he knew so well his brother's ardent spirit and rashness.

Before daybreak they all set out for the ford, with the Arab marching at their head, and went out of the straight road to avoid being seen by their foes. The Arab plunged into the water first of all, and as he knew the way perfectly it was not difficult for him to cross, but Robert of Artois did not find it so easy to effect a footing, the opposite shore being high and slippery from the richness of its soil. Next to him went the Templars, and then William, Earl of Salisbury, surnamed "Longue Epée," who had joined the crusade with two hundred English knights. Ah! little those brave men knew they were going to their death, and that of all who crossed in hope and ardour that morning, only enough should survive to come back and tell the tale!

The sight of the Arabs fleeing who guarded the ford, made Robert forget the oath he had sworn to his brother; he rushed after them in pursuit; the Emir Facardin coming out to ascertain the cause of alarm, was quickly surrounded and killed, and numbers of the Saracens, in dismay at the loss of their leader, left their camp to their foes, and retired in disorder to Massoura.

Meanwhile the king had passed the ford in his turn, with all the rest of the horsemen, and was greatly surprised that he did not find his brother and the advance guard waiting for him on the other side. Fearing some misfortune had happened, he told ten of his knights to go in search of Count Robert, and remind him that he was to attempt nothing until the whole army had assembled. After this he set out quickly in the direction of the

Saracens; but what was his astonishment when he found that instead of being able to stand against them, he was surrounded by them on all sides, whilst the air was filled with their hideous cries, and the noise of their barbarous instruments! The Saracens, terror-stricken at first by the approach of the Christians, had now rallied in multitudes, and completely closed in the army of the crusaders between the river and the town of Massoura. The king, undismayed, prepared for immediate battle, although his knights and nobles tried to persuade him that it would be hopeless to combat so large a force. Just at that moment the constable Imbert de Beaujeu rode up to tell him that the Count of Artois was besieged in a house at Massoura, and would perish if succour did not arrive. The king sent a body of troops to his aid, and promised that he would soon be with him himself; and then he turned to his people and exhorted them to keep their ranks firm; and told them that the soldiers of Christ ought not to fear a set of miscreants like those who were crowding around them. The whole aspect of the king that day inspired courage; his face was calm, his eyes shone with a steadfast light; he had a helmet of gold on his head, which from his great height towered above the ranks of his army; his double-edged sword was so heavy, that to strike a blow with it, he had to grasp it with both hands.

The signal being given, the bravest of the crusaders rushed on the Saracens; others, less courageous, tried to regain the camp of the Duke of Burgundy, but were most of them drowned in the attempt. The king was sure to be found where the fight was the thickest, or where the weak were in want of succour; and once during the battle he was surrounded by six Saracens, who seized the bridle of his horse, and yet he freed himself by his own aid alone.

The Duke of Burgundy and his men heard the conflict going on from the opposite shore; they longed to fly to the king's assistance, but their very eagerness hindered them, and it was a long time before any of them could cross the river. When a body of the king's archers arrived on the plain, they found that Louis had maintained his ground, and that the battle of Massoura was won: yet, had it not been for the king's example, the day had been lost, so great was the fury and strength of the enemy.

Both Christians and Saracens were now utterly wearied out with fighting; the heat had been intense, and Louis, having waited for all the wounded who could be assembled, set out at sunset for the Saracen camp on the Thanis. His golden helmet oppressed him, and he was glad to accept from Joinville a casque of steel, which enabled him to breathe more freely. He had only gone a little way on the road when a prior of the knights hospitallers met him and asked if he knew where his brother was, the Count of Artois.

"Yes," replied the king, "I know that he is in heaven." And then he said that the Lord should be praised equally for what He gave and for what He withheld; and in the dark of the evening his tears began to flow, not only for his own sorrow, but for that of the young Countess of Artois, who had only come out to the East to bid her husband a last farewell.

For Robert indeed was slain; deaf to the remonstrances of the Grand Master of the Templars, an old man, whose advice had been well heeded, and to those of the Earl of Salisbury, he persisted in following the Saracens to Massoura, and had met there the fate he had drawn upon him by his untimely zeal and rashness. His brave companions perished with him, with the exception of the Grand Master, who lost an eye in the conflict, and one or two others; the Englishman who bore the standard wrapped it around him as he fell. And as the king appeared to have known beforehand what had happened, so it is said the mother of the Earl of Salisbury had a vision of her son ascending to heaven, with a crown of glory on his head, before she received the tidings of his death.

The king encamped that night close by the machines of the Saracens, and on the second day after the battle of Massoura, the struggle began afresh. The Saracens had taken the victory to themselves, and had sent the news of their supposed triumph to Cairo by their carrier pigeons. Bondocar, the chief, who had rallied the troops in Massoura appeared on the field in the coat of arms starred with lilies which Robert of Artois had worn. The Greek fire was poured forth incessantly from the front line of the Saracens as they came up in battle array; the king had the crupper of his horse covered with it once during the conflict, when he had gone to the rescue of his brother Charles, who was in danger. The Saracens were repulsed a second time, but the victory was dearly bought, so many men and horses being wounded, and the crusaders passed a dreary time before Massoura, whilst their provisions grew less and less; and it being Lent, they lost their strength by eating only roots, wheat, and fruit; fish they had in plenty at first, but to their horror they found out that they had fed on the dead bodies which the Saracens had thrown into the river. A pestilence broke out, and the camp was like one vast hospital. The king, in mistaken zeal, had caused the bodies to be taken out of the water, that those of the Christians might receive Christian burial, and helped to bury them himself. This only increased the unwholesomeness of the air, and at last Louis fell ill too. The crusaders now began to despair; the king had been as brave in misfortune as he had been on the battle-field, and had cheered the spirits of his followers: he visited the sick day and night, and sat beside the bedside of the dying, reminding them of their Saviour's love, and comforting many a poor soul with the hope of heaven. It is recorded how one of the lowliest of the army declared as he lay dying that he could not depart until he had seen the kind face of his master bending over him once more.

The Saracens having prevented the approach of the vessels that were coming to the camp with provisions, the king, as a last resource, offered to give up the city of Damietta to the Sultan Malek al Moadhem, if he would agree to restore Jerusalem to the Christians, the Counts of Poiton and Anjou remaining in Egypt as hostages.

The Sultan would have no other hostage but the king himself, and Louis would willingly have sacrificed himself for his people if his nobles had allowed him to do so. There was no alternative but to retreat to Damietta, and the army decamped one spring night in the dark, the old people and the sick and wounded being carried out first, and the king leaving the camp the last of all with the barons Gautier de Chatillon and Geoffray de Sardines. He was so weak and ill that he could hardly sit upright on his little Arab horse; yet he was the bravest among the brave in that troop which went slowly and sadly along in the dark, defending themselves as they could from the attacks of the Arabs, who had been bribed for the purpose of molesting them.

Geoffray de Sardines had to deal many a blow to keep the Saracens from his master, who soon became too feeble to lift his sword, and they were in the greater danger because the whole of the Egyptian army was behind them. At last they reached a little village, and the king, having fainted away, was carried into the first house they met with, whilst Chatillon stood outside in the street defending it until he fell mortally wounded.

When Louis had recovered a little, Philip de Montfort came to him, and told him that he had seen an emir, to whom he had been sent on a mission once before, and if he liked he would make a treaty with him on the terms desired by the Saracens.

The king agreed to the plan; De Montfort went to the emir, and all would have been well if a sergeant belonging to the French army, thinking to save the king's life, had not cried out to the knights who were standing around, "Surrender, Sir Knights! the king commands you to do so!" The Christian warriors, believing that the king had really commanded them to give way, lay down their swords, and the emir, seeing they were all prisoners, said there was no further need of a treaty. Then cords and chains were thrown around them, and they were all conducted to Massoura.

The king was shut up in the house of a scribe; he was loaded with chains, and strictly watched, while the barons and knights were huddled together in a court which was open to the sky. King Louis was very unkindly treated by the Sultan at first; he was only allowed to have one attendant with him;

this man, whose name was Isambert, nursed him tenderly, dressed him, and made his bread; and said afterwards that he had never heard his master utter one word of complaint or impatience during the whole time of his captivity. It was a marvel how Louis ever lived through his illness; his strength was almost spent; and at night, to add to his discomfort, he had nothing to cover him as he lay on his wretched bed but an old cloak, which a poor man had given him out of compassion in Massoura.

After a time, Malek al Moadhem, fearing the reproaches of the European nations, treated his captive more kindly; he had his chains removed and sent him his own physicians, and delicate food from his royal table, and to keep him warm he gave him two robes of black samite, trimmed and lined with fur, which were plentifully adorned with gold buttons. And best of all he allowed him to have his almoner and a priest with him, and something like joy came back to the poor king when the Saracens brought him one day his missal, or book of prayers, which he had lost and never thought to see again. And so, comforted and strengthened by prayer, Louis was not unhappy even within prison walls, away from all he loved, and waited patiently until the Almighty should see fit to make a way for him to regain his liberty.

And a way came at last: the sultan agreed to release him on condition of his giving up Damietta and paying a ransom of a million besants of gold. Louis agreed to the terms, but he said that the liberty of the King of France should not be bought with money, and that the gold should be paid for his people, and the city should be his own ransom. The sultan, struck with the spirit of his reply, reduced the sum he had asked by two hundred thousand besants, and a truce was concluded between the Christians and the Saracens of Egypt and Syria. It was arranged that half the ransom should be paid at once, and the other half as soon as the king should reach the port of Acre in Palestine, his brother Alphonse remaining in Egypt as hostage. Louis was then set at liberty; he had recovered from his illness through the skill of the Arabian physicians, and he repaired to Acre where the queen and the princesses had already arrived, having quitted Damietta a little while before. It was a joyful meeting, for Marguerite had been very unhappy through all those long sad months at Damietta, not only on account of the miseries of the crusaders, but also from the constant fear of falling into the hands of the Saracens herself. And a little son who was born to her there received the name of "Tristan," in memory of the sorrows she had endured.

Louis did not return to France at once, but remained some time at Acre, in the hope of inducing the Christian powers to enter into a league for the recovery of the Holy Land, and it was not until the news of his mother's death reached him, and his presence was required in his country, that he bade farewell to the East, where he had bravely striven for so much, and yet had gained so little.

The king was received with great joy by his people on his return to France, but they were less happy when they saw the cross still on his shoulder, as a sign that he meant to engage in another crusade when the truce should have expired. As soon as he arrived he occupied himself in making good laws for his country, and was so greatly famed for his justice that other sovereigns were glad to benefit by his example. His laws against evil-doers were very severe; no murderer or thief dared abide in Paris, and merchants and tradesmen who gave false measures were punished with extreme rigour. The king used often to sit beneath an oak in the Bois de Vincennes, or on a carpet spread in a garden, to hear the complaints and grievances of the common people, and to administer justice to them. He had always been charitable from his earliest years: a hundred and twenty poor persons were maintained in his house, and three poor old men, besides those who were crippled and lame, dined with him every day at his own table; the king would cut their bread and meat for them, and pour out their wine, and would serve them before he ate anything himself. And beyond this, he gave large sums to hospitals, religious houses, and colleges, and succoured widows and poor ladies and gentlemen, and all those who by reason of age or illness could no longer work for their living.

The good king used to employ the morning with the affairs of the state; he dined at mid-day, and after dinner his readers would come to him, and he read the Bible with interpreters, or the works of the fathers of the church: sometimes, instead of reading, he would converse with good and learned men, who always found a welcome at his court. In the evening, before he retired to rest, he used to assemble his children around him, and hear them repeat their prayers and the tasks they had learned during the day. Then he would tell them of the deeds of good emperors and kings, and of the fate that generally befel those who were idle, or careless of the happiness of their subjects. At midnight he would rise from his bed to attend Matins, and so afraid was he of being asleep when any of the church services began, that he had candles lighted which only burnt a certain time, that his servants might not fail to awaken him as soon as they were spent. His brothers used to share with him works of charity and holy offices. When Baldwin II., Emperor of Constantinople, sent him as a gift the Crown of Thorns supposed to be the one worn by our blessed Saviour, and part of the word of the True Cross on which He died, in return for the aid Louis had afforded him when he was in great need, we read how the king received the sacred relics in the deepest humility, and bareheaded and barefoot carried the Crown of Thorns with his brother Robert of Artois to the church of Notre-Dame. It was to form a shrine for these relics that Louis built the beautiful Sainte Chapelle in Paris. Again, we read how, when a new hospital was completed, the king carried in the first bed himself, with his son-in-law, the King of Navarre, whilst his brothers conveyed the remainder of the sick people into the wards. The whole family were united in deeds of love and compassion. There was no office too lowly for Louis to perform; no person, however mean and wretched, who had not a place in his heart. And if we except the harsh laws he made against the Jews through his zeal for the Christian faith, no sovereign ever showed more mercy and justice towards his people.

One Good Friday, when the king was going his rounds to all the churches in Paris, according to his custom, he saw on the other side of the way a leper who was shunned by every person he met. The king immediately crossed over the muddy road and gave the poor man some money, and kissed his hand to show that he loved him, although he was despised and avoided by all others. The king never resumed his costly robes after his return from the Holy Land, but wore dark-coloured garments of cloth and silk, and instead of handsome furs he only wore the skins of hares, rabbits, and squirrels, that he might have the more money to spare for his charities.

In the summer of the year 1270 the Christians set out once more from the port of Aigues-Mortes on the seventh and last crusade. Bondocar had become a very powerful sovereign, and the Saracens were making so great progress in the East, that all Christian princes became alarmed, and were urged by the Pope to hasten to the relief of Palestine.

The Crusaders, with Louis and three of his sons at their head, directed their course this time to Tunis, hoping by gaining possession of that city to cut off all communication between the Saracens of the East, and those of Morocco and Spain.

As soon as they arrived before Tunis the enemy came in sight, as if they were going to attack the camp, and then retired. Just as they were vanishing in the distance two Spanish slaves came and told the king that the Lord of Tunis had arrested all who were Christians amongst his troops, and intended to cut off their heads directly the march should begin upon Tunis. The next night three Saracens appeared before the advance guard of the Christians, and touching their turbans in token of respect, made known by signs that they demanded baptism.

The king did not know what to think of the matter, and ordered them to be guarded in a tent; and a little while after a hundred more appeared, making the same signs. Whilst they were amusing the soldiers by their odd gestures, other Saracens rushed unexpectedly upon the camp, and after killing many of the Christians, ran away before they could be captured. The army thought to revenge the affront on the three men, but they began to shed tears, and one of them declared that a captain of more than two thousand men like himself wanted to ruin him by treachery, and if the king would send one of the two others to the camp of the Saracens, the whole army would pass over to the Christians. The king did not dare to trust him, and thought it wisest to send them all away, for fear he should be guilty of shedding innocent blood. As the Crusaders were making a very deep ditch the next day all around the camp, the entire body of the Saracens came in sight, spreading from the sea on one side, to the country on the other. They meant to surround the army, but Louis rushing out upon them, a skirmish ensued, and when a few of their number were slain, all the rest took flight. Thus they kept on harassing and dodging the army; the Christian warriors had no peace with them; and if ever they took off their armour they had to put it on again directly for some fresh alarm, although the Saracens never ventured to give them battle.

Louis was desirous of waiting before Tunis until the arrival of his brother Charles, now king over Sicily; and he prepared meanwhile by sea and land for the siege of the city, which was very strongly fortified. The delay proved the source of misfortune; the Christians had worse evils to contend with than those occasioned by the Saracens. The heat was intense, and the reflection from the sunlit mountains caused a dazzling light which almost blinded their eyes. When the wind blew it came loaded with burning sand, and the plague broke out on the coast. Then the Crusaders drooped one by one; the young Count de Nevers, the son whom Louis loved best of all, was seized with the sickness and died, and on the day of his death the good Saint Louis fell ill himself. When he felt that he should never rise from his bed again, he set all his earthly affairs in order, and gave good advice to his children, telling them always to love one another, and maintain the peace of their country. For the rest of the time he lived he prayed in patience, and praised God for all that had befallen him throughout his life; and one night he uttered the word "Jerusalem," adding, "Let us go to Jerusalem." It was to the heavenly Jerusalem the king was going, the eternal city, where all weeping and sorrow and trouble should be hushed for ever. Before he died he prayed long and earnestly for his people, that they might be delivered from their enemies, and last of all, with peace in his face, he lifted up his eyes to heaven and said, "Lord, I will enter into Thy house; I will adore Thee in Thy holy temple, and I will glorify Thy name."

When Charles of Anjou arrived at Tunis a little while after the king had ceased to breathe, he was surprised to find that the camp was all silent, and that no one had come to meet him on the shore. And hastening to the royal tent, the sight that greeted him was the dead body of his brother clad in a hair shirt, and stretched on a bed of ashes; for thus had Louis, in his humility, desired to die. Charles shed many tears, and kissed the feet of his dead brother again and again, and the whole camp was filled with sorrowful faces, so dearly had the good king been loved by his followers.

Louis, having reigned over France for nearly forty-four years, left the kingdom to his eldest son Philip, who carried on the crusade for a while with the other princes, and defeated the Saracens on several occasions. By November, however, all the French Crusaders had quitted the East, and Philip occupied himself in the affairs of his own country. His father wrote him some instructions, which he was to read after his death, and which have been carefully preserved. The following maxims were amongst those they contained:—

> "Dear son, the first thing I teach thee is to set thy heart to love God, for without Him none can be saved.
>
> "If God send thee adversity, receive it with patience, and thank the Lord for it, and think that thou hast deserved it, and that it will turn to thy profit. If He give thee prosperity, thank Him for it humbly, so as not to lose by pride or otherwise what ought to render thee better; for one ought not to abuse the gifts of God."
>
> "Be kind and charitable to the poor, the weak, and those who are in trouble, and aid them according to thy power."
>
> "Maintain the good customs of thy country, and destroy the bad ones. Only have in thy company prudent and unambitious men. Flee and avoid the company of the wicked."
>
> "Listen willingly to the word of God, and keep it in thy heart. Let no one be so bold as to speak a word which might lead to sin in thy presence."

GUSTAVUS VASA, KING OF SWEDEN

There was once a princess named Margaret, daughter of Waldemar, King of Denmark, who on her father's death married Haquin, king of Norway. When her husband died she reigned over Norway alone; and when her son Olaus died she reigned over Denmark too. Margaret governed her people well, but she dearly loved power, and was not content with the countries she already possessed; so she went to war with her near neighbours, the Swedes, and defeated and captured Albert, their king. Margaret kept him in prison seven years, and then only released him when he had agreed to give up his crown as the price of his liberty. In the year 1397 a great meeting of the States General of the three countries was held at a place called Calmar, and there it was settled that Denmark, Sweden, and Norway, should all be governed by one sovereign. After Margaret's death the Swedes were very unhappy for many years, because they were so sorely oppressed by the Danes: they did not submit tamely, and a long series of troubles and wars ensued.

When Gustavus Vasa, the great hero of the North, was born in the year 1490, Sweden had in some measure freed itself from the Danish yoke, and was governed by Sten Sture, a Swede, who had the title of Adminstrator. Sture was a man of firm and upright character, who had never suffered the Danes to triumph over him, although they were always trying to regain full power over his country, and had made a solemn vow with the Russians to subdue it entirely.

Gustavus Erickson, commonly called Gustavus Vasa, was born at the Castle of Lindholm, near Stockholm. His father, Erick Johannson, was descended from the royal houses of Vasa and Sture, both of which came from the Old Norwegian kings, and were connected with many of the royal families of Europe. They had always been renowned for their love of freedom, their steadfast spirit, and their valour. Sten Sture had given to Erick Johannson a beautiful estate, called Castle-holm, and the Island of Aland, in the Gulf of Bothnia. He loved to have him with him at his court, and took charge of his little son Gustavus, because he wanted to see him grow up worthy of his royal birth, and to teach him to love his unhappy country with all his heart; hoping that he might one day restore to it the freedom it had enjoyed before it was overcome by the ambitious Northern queen.

The boy was brought up simply and without luxury; he ate coarse food, and learned to hunt, and was allowed to climb about the mountains around Lindholm as much as he liked, so that he grew very strong, and could endure great fatigue without a murmur, whilst he thoroughly enjoyed his sports and his liberty in the keen, fresh air. When John, the reigning king of Denmark came in State to visit Sture at Stockholm, he was struck by the spirited bearing, and free, open nature of Gustavus; and fearing that when he was older he might prove the source of danger to himself, he asked Sture to let him take care of him, and bring him up at the Danish court. Sture, however, wisely declined his offer, and sent the child to Aland to be out of danger, and watched over him until his death, when Svante Sture governed Sweden in his place. Gustavus was treated with great kindness by the new Administrator, who loved peace, and only suffered good men to be around him, thus making his Court a school for all knightly virtues. Gustavus remained with him until he was eighteen, and then went to Upsal to attend a school which had been founded there by the elder Sture. A story is told of him which shows how deeply the teaching of his friend had taken root in his heart. In one of the divisions of the school he was accustomed to read the classics with a Dane, who once happened to let fall some remarks against Sweden. In a moment, the Swedish youth drew his sword, plunged it through the book which was open before him, and rushed out of the place, never to return to it again. For all this, he was very happy at Upsal, and they were merry days when a flock of students, in their red gowns, rushed out of the city gates to enjoy a holiday in the open country beyond. Gustavus studied with great diligence, and was more learned than most of the other noble youths of his time, for in general they were quite content if they knew how to handle their weapons, and cared very little for learning out of books. Gustavus made himself perfect in all knightly accomplishments, and could play on several musical instruments, which were all kept long afterwards, hung up in the Castle of Stockholm, in remembrance of the happy days of his youth. He never touched them after he had once given his whole thought to the rescue of his country, but I dare say, when his great work was done, and Sweden was free and happy once more, and he looked at them as they hung on the walls, he seemed to hear all the old tunes which had gladdened his youth, and thought kindly of the companions of his early years, who had many of them died, or passed out of his sight.

Gustavus was tall, slender, and fairhaired; his countenance was open and expressed kindness; his temper was cheerful, and his courage could never be daunted: he had a wonderful memory to the very last hours of his life. When he had been in Upsal six years he came back to the Court of Stockholm, where he went on with his studies, and lived until he was twenty-five years of age, beloved by his friends, and esteemed by all for his upright conduct.

In the meantime a change had taken place in the affairs of Denmark. King John was dead, and his son Christiern the Second had come to the throne. The new king suffered himself to be advised by his mother-in-law Sigbritt, a spiteful and meddling Dutchwoman; and he began his reign with many unjust actions towards the Swedes, which provoked them to fight once more for their freedom. Sten Sture the younger had succeeded his father Svante; he resolved to free his country from the bondage of Denmark, and he spoke earnest words in the Council House.

"We must be firm," he said. "We must offer up our blood, and show the people who come after us, how dear to us was our freedom, rather than sit still with a weight upon our shoulders, which crushes us to the ground."

And very soon the war began. King Christiern came himself to the scene of action, and lay siege to Stockholm. Sture and Gustavus Erickson, who bore the banner of Sweden, gained two victories over the Danes; the king was in danger, being nearly surrounded by his enemies, and was obliged to think of returning to his own country. He made it appear as if he wished for peace, and agreed to meet Sture in order to treat for terms, provided hostages were sent to his quarters in the persons of Gustavus and five Swedish statesmen of high rank. It was arranged that when these hostages reached his vessel at a place called Krongshamm, he should present himself in the quarters of Sture, and that when he returned to his vessel the Swedes should be free to depart.

Although it was well known that the promises of Christiern were not to be trusted, the six hostages set out in a boat with a crew of twelve men, but they had hardly got half-way when a Danish vessel, having a hundred men on board, met them, and closed their path. The captain told them that the king wished to meet them at a place called Elfsnabbe, where he had some important matters to discuss with them. Gustavus replied with spirit that they had simply come as hostages, and had no power to transact business; they would therefore either await the king at Krongshamm or return at once to their own quarters.

The Swedes soon found, however, that it was of no use to resist, and they were forced on board the Danish vessel, and thus conveyed to the king. The tyrant rejoiced that he had Gustavus Vasa, the most dreaded of his enemies in his power, and without taking any heed of his promise, sailed with his booty to Denmark as quickly as he could. The people of

Sweden were very sorrowful, and angry too when they knew Gustavus had been thus captured, for his brave conduct and his success had already made them hope that better days were in store for them. Sture also was grieved at Christiern's breach of faith—the more so that he had been too generous to suspect him of such deceit—and only a short time before, when the king had been brought very low by sickness and famine, had sent him succour, and cared for him as if he had been his warmest friend instead of his most bitter foe.

When the Swedes arrived in Denmark they were shut up in the citadel of Copenhagen, and it was decided that they should be put to death at once. Only, as they had been guilty of no crime, it was not easy to find a pretence for passing sentence upon them. Whilst their fate was pending, Sigbritt urged the king to spare their lives, saying, that so long as he had them in his power, he could impose upon the Swedes laws more and more severe, with the threat of putting their countrymen to instant death if they did not obey them. Christiern, as usual, followed the advice of his mother-in-law, which for once proved the source of blessing to Sweden, and Gustavus and his companions were only shut up in prison.

Gustavus had a kinsman at Copenhagen of the name of Banner, who was much attached to him, and feared that if he lived solely under the eye of the tyrant he would be exposed to many insults. So he prevailed with Christiern to let him keep him in his castle of Calloë, a strong fortress in Denmark, and made himself a surety for him to the amount of six thousand dollars.

In the early part of the year 1520 Christiern declared war. The Swedes were prepared to resist him, for the peasants had come down from the mountains, and had flocked to the standard of Sture until the army was increased to the number of 10,000 men. The cause of the king of Denmark was strongly favoured by the Pope and Trolle, Archbishop of Upsal, who were both very angry because the Protestant faith was daily gaining ground in Sweden. Trolle came of an ancient house, only second in rank and dignity to that of Sture, and a long standing quarrel between these two houses served at the present moment to widen the breach between them.

The Swedes fought bravely, but they were soon overcome, and in a battle at Bogisund, Sture received a wound in the head, of which he died a few days after. The state of the country now seemed hopeless; its regular army only numbered 500 men; those who had crowded its ranks when the war began were brave-hearted men, eager to defend the right, but they were not trained and skilful soldiers. Sture dead, and Gustavus Vasa in prison, there was neither ruler in the land nor leader in strife. The Swedes began indeed to be disheartened; a few of the bravest clung to the hope that a fresh attempt might yet be made to resist the tyrant's power; some, less hopeful, thought it best to lay down their swords and submit; others again, said that they would rather die first. Sture's widow, Christina—herself of royal birth—and a woman of great spirit, came forward to revenge her husband's death, and to implore the Swedes not to desert the cause of freedom. She sent her little son Nil Sture to Dantzig to be out of danger, and went to Stockholm, where she made the people swear rather to bury themselves beneath the ruins of the city, than become the slaves of the Danish king.

For a short time a little gleam of hope broke over the land, but Christiern feeling assured that he could not really call himself King of Sweden until he had Stockholm in his power, resolved to come in person with a great fleet and besiege the capital.

In the meantime Gustavus was sorrowing for the troubles of his fatherland, and his face was clouded and sad when he followed his kinsman Banner to the gay festivals of the Danish court, and heard people tell how the king had triumphed over his countrymen, and was bending by degrees their proud spirit. He was heartily tired, too, of his prison, although he was guarded less strictly now than he had been at first, and was allowed to wander about by himself within one mile of the castle. During his lonely walks he revolved many plans in his mind, and at last one morning at sunrise he put on the disguise of a peasant, and made his escape from Calloë. The first day he wandered about a part of the country unknown to him, and the next day at noon he reached the town of Flensburg, where he feared he should have been betrayed. But outside the town, for his good fortune, he found a number of Saxon merchants who had been buying oxen in Jutland, and were on their way back to Germany; without much trouble he entered their service, and thus got safely out of Denmark.

In the September of the year 1519 he came to the free city of Lubeck, where he made himself known at the Council House, and asked to be received as a guest, secure from the tyranny of the Danish king. Soon after he arrived, Banner came in search of him. He was very angry with Gustavus for having escaped out of his hands, and exposed him to the king's wrath, and wanted him to return with him to Denmark. Gustavus promised to refund the six thousand dollars Banner would be obliged to forfeit, but it was not likely that he would agree to go back to his gloomy prison. So he remained some months at Lubeck, and heard there of the death of Sture and the defeat of his countrymen. It was at this time, when Martin Luther, the great Reformer, came to visit the city of Lubeck, that Gustavus Vasa declared himself a convert to the Protestant faith.

The Council at last promised to assist him with men and money, and granted him a merchant's vessel in which he reached the coast of Sweden towards the end of May in the year 1520. As he approached Stockholm, he found its haven filled by the Danish fleet, and not caring to show himself yet, he landed at a promontory a short distance from Calmar. Stockholm was now possessed by the Danes, King Christiern had taken up his abode in one of the palaces, and Christina had been forced to retire to the castle, which was strongly guarded, and still held out against the Danes. Gustavus entered the city secretly and found his way to the castle, where he was welcomed and received with great honour by Sture's widow. He then went to the market place, and made himself known to the people who had assembled there in crowds, and he told them what a disgrace it was for them to be in bondage to Christiern. The people listened in silence and hung their heads; it seemed as if all spirit had been crushed within them. So Gustavus went back to the castle to see if he could arouse a better feeling there, but the German soldiers who were employed to guard it broke out into fury at the very idea of fighting, they were so utterly tired of all the misery of war, and they would have murdered Gustavus on the spot if Christina had not been there to protect him.

He now saw that his only safety would be at the head of an army: the Danes were all ready to besiege the castle, and it was therefore no longer a place to shelter him; but the moment for action was not yet come, and he roamed about in the country around Stockholm in disguise, now in the forests and now in the fields, hiding by day and travelling by night, and mingling sometimes with the Danes for the purpose of gaining news. And on Sundays, when the peasants were in the churches, he would stand amongst them, and try to cheer them by telling them that happier days were in store for them when they should be free once more. Still the people did not care to listen: they said that so long as they obeyed the King of Denmark, they had salt and herrings in plenty; what more did they want? And sometimes when Gustavus had turned away from them they would shoot after him with their arrows. Such was the abject state they had been brought to by long-continued insult and oppression. Besides this Christiern had spies in all parts, and had set a heavy price upon the head of Gustavus, and threatened all persons who should attempt to conceal him with the punishment of death.

After escaping from many dangers, he came through Ludermannland to the house of Joachim Brahe, a noble councillor of Sweden, who had married his sister Margaret. The meeting between brother and sister was full of joy, and Gustavus hoped that Brahe would have been prevailed upon to take up arms in the defence of his country, but the prudent statesman was not to be enticed. Christiern, whose presence had for a time been required in Denmark, was now on his way to Stockholm, and Brahe was one of the guests invited thither to behold the crown of Sweden placed upon his head. He could see nothing but rashness and certain failure in the project of taking up arms against so powerful a foe. Gustavus, therefore, bade his sister farewell with a heavy heart, and went on his way once more, and after wandering about some time longer in disguise, he retired to a country house at Rafnäes, which belonged to his father, to think over in solitude what was best to be done.

King Christiern arrived in Stockholm with his wife, leaving Sigbritt to manage the affairs of Denmark. With the help of the Pope, and the Archbishop of Upsal, he had himself declared heir to the Swedish throne before an immense concourse of people, and was crowned in their presence. Before this he promised to release all captives, and conferred many marks of royal favour upon the chief men of Stockholm. The first days after he was crowned were given up to knightly sports, and feasting, and merriment. But before three days had passed, the king's cruel temper got the better of him, and he withdrew from the scene of rejoicing to a secret council chamber, where he sat thinking over the best means of getting rid of the bishops and senators, and all men of high estate in Sweden, that his own position on the throne might be quite secure.

Soon it appeared as if a shadow of gloom had fallen over the city, where all had been noisy mirth: the castle was suddenly filled with prisoners; bishops and statesmen were alike consigned to its dark dungeons; in all the market places scaffolds were erected; and the unhappy captives were told that they must die.

The 8th of November in the year 1520 was the day on which the fearful deed began, a deed never equalled in horror in the annals of Swedish history. Early in the dark morning all the gates of the city were shut to prevent anybody from taking flight, and making the affair known in the country beyond. Every new comer was let in, but no one was allowed to go out. The streets were guarded, and field-pieces were placed upon the great market place, levelled towards the people. The way from the castle to the market was lined with Danish soldiers; trumpeters rode about the streets and proclaimed that all persons were to retire to their houses; and close their doors on pain of death. But the common people were horror-struck at these preparations they dared to disobey the king's orders, and crowded together to see what would happen next.

Towards noon the castle gates were opened, and bishops and nobles, councillors and burgomasters, were led between executioners and common soldiers to the appointed place on the market, just in front of the Council House. The bishops were clad in their sacred robes, the councillors had not had time to take off the dress they wore in council. Oh what a sad procession it was, as they came slowly along, with erect heads and a proud and calm demeanour worthy of their race! Sobs and murmurs were heard amongst the crowd; the roughest of the soldiers and headsmen were touched with pity and respect as these innocent men, most of them grey-headed, walked to their death. As soon as they reached the market place, a speech was made to the mob in which it was declared that the king was deeply grieved to be obliged to have recourse to such severe measures, but that he felt himself bound to punish the Swedes for the offence they had given to the Pope by becoming Protestants. And thus he made the terrible crime he was about to commit even worse, by his falsehood!

One of the bishops, an aged man, then declared his innocence, and asked that a clergyman might be allowed to attend himself and his companions in their last moments; but his request was refused, and a noise was made to prevent his words from being heard by the people. Then the headsmen began their dread work; the fourth victim was Erick Johannson the father of Gustavus. In a little time the market place was filled with dead bodies and the streets streamed with blood. Some of the mob, roused to a state of frenzy by the dreadful spectacle, made an attempt to rescue those of the doomed ones who were yet living, but they were cut down by the soldiers who had received orders to quell any outbreak on the part of the common people with the punishment of death. Escape was not to be thought of, because the gates of the city were always kept closed; the frightened people crept into cellars and corners. And when the king heard that they had hidden themselves, he caused a decree of pardon to be read, so that many of them came out believing it to be true, and only fell into the trap he had thus artfully laid for them.

Ninety-four Swedes fell the first day. For two days and two nights the corpses lay on the market place, and the cattle and the fowls strayed amongst them. To add to the horror the king caused the dead bodies of Sture the younger and his son Sten to be disinterred and thrown amongst the murdered to be buried with them.

Sture's widow, Christina, did not escape the king's wrath; she was summoned to his presence and condemned to die, but some persons present asked the tyrant to spare her life, and she was only sentenced to be imprisoned for the rest of her days.

In other parts of Sweden deeds equally cruel were enacted. Numbers of the peasants were deprived each of a leg and a hand, and, thus maimed, they were supposed to be able to till the land although they could not possibly fight. For these acts of cruelty and oppression Christiern the Second justly gained the title of the Wicked, and his own people soon began to hate him as much as the Swedes hated him for all the evil he had done.

In the meantime Gustavus was sought for in vain. He was still in his hiding-place at Rafnäes, sending out his peasants now and then to collect news. And one sad day a grey-haired man came to the neighbouring castle of Gripsholm which belonged to Joachim Brahe. It was Brahe's steward; he had followed his master to Stockholm, and had witnessed his unhappy fate. The old man could not speak for crying, and could only make known by signs the terrible events that had happened. Soon after, a peasant came by, and told the same story. And Gustavus sat in the lonely house, sorrowing for his father and his friends, and many of his kindred besides; yet although he was forsaken by all, and surrounded as it were by enemies, he would not give up hope, but only longed the more to succour his unhappy country. So one day he packed up all the money and valuable things he possessed, and taking them with him, left Rafnäes on horseback with the idea of persuading the brave people of Dalecarlia to stand by him in the struggle for freedom.

This province, which was the scene of his adventures for some time, is bordered on its western side by Norway: the mountain ridge which divides the sources of its two rivers Dalef from Lake Fämund in that country rises to between three and four thousand feet above the level of the sea. Dalecarlia abounds in rivers and lakes; the winters there are long and severe; corn will not grow, and the tender bark of the pine trees is mixed with the scanty supply of rye or barley of which the people make their bread. Wolves and bears frequent the forests, and fish is plentiful in all the lakes, except in those near Fahlun, now the capital of the province, where the vapours for ever rising out of the great copper mine there, drive away to a distance birds, beasts, and fishes, and destroy, all verdure in the country around. Fahlun lies in a wide valley between two lakes; the mine is a vast abyss, and is worked open to the sky, and besides copper produces gold, silver, vitriol, ochre, and brimstone. The natives of Darlecarlia are hardy from the nature of their climate; they have always been very brave, trusting in their own strength, and having very little intercourse with the other people of Sweden. At the time Gustavus was amongst them they were so simple in their manners that the noblemen could scarcely be distinguished from the peasants. There was not a town then in the whole province, the people clustered together in villages, which were divided into parishes. Some of these lay along the rivers and lakes, others were hidden among the mountains, and were only to be approached by the steepest and most difficult of paths.

Gustavus took with him as he supposed the most faithful of all his servants, but the cowardly man thought the fortunes of his master much too insecure to be followed, and contrived to get away from him with the valuable things it had been his duty to carry. Gustavus soon found out his treachery, and pursued him until his horse could go no farther; then, being in great danger himself, he was obliged to leave the horse and the few things he had with him on the road and run for very life. Thus, without friends or money, clad in a coarse peasant's frock, he wandered about the dark pine forests and the mountains, only occasionally finding a roof to shelter his head from the inclement winter nights, or food to satisfy his sharp hunger. Still he never despaired, but trusted that God would let him live until he should have given back to his country the happiness it had lost for so long.

On the last day of November he arrived at Fahlun, and there he cut his hair short, and put on a round hat, such as the Dalecarlians wore, and a rough woollen vest, and set out with an axe on his shoulder in search of work. In a little time he found employment in the mines of Fahlun, by which he earned barely enough for his support; and finding that the noxious vapours and the closeness of the mines impaired his health, he left them, and wandered farther until he came to the house of a rich man named Andres Fehrson. Here he was hired as a farm-labourer, and set to work in the barns. The other farm-servants soon began to watch the new comer with interest. In their intercourse with him they soon found that he was not quite like one of themselves; he had been observed, too, to wear a rich silken handkerchief, beneath his woollen vest, and they suspected that he was some nobleman in disguise. Reports of this reached the ears of Fehrson, and he desired that the stranger should come to him. The very moment he saw him he recognised him as a fellow student in the school at Upsal, but although he was very glad to see his old comrade again, he dared not keep so dangerous a person in his house, and he urged him to go higher up the mountains and not to stay too long a time in one place. Gustavus was therefore obliged to set out on his wearisome travels once more: the winter had set in with all its rigour, the lakes and rivers were frozen, and as he was crossing some ice between Wika and Torsanga, a part of it gave way, and he fell up to his shoulders in the water, and was very nearly drowned. However, he managed to clamber out, and he found his way to a cottage, where some kind peasants gave him food and shelter, and afterwards brought him to the country house of Arendt Fehrson, a relation of Andres, who had served under Gustavus in the war with the Danes.

This man appeared to receive him with respect and courtesy, but soon after his arrival he rode swiftly to one of his friends to tell him of the prize concealed in his house, and to ask him to join him in making the affair known to the king;—for it will be remembered that a heavy price had been set upon the head of Gustavus—and the man who would have been base enough to betray him would have reaped great gain to himself. This friend was too honourable to listen to such a proposal, and Fehrson, enraged at his refusal, went to another of his friends, an officer in the Danish service, who had fewer scruples. Fehrson passed the evening at his house in feasting and drinking, and it was planned between them that he should return home the next morning, accompanied by twenty men, and seize the fugitive by force.

But Barbro Stigsdotter, the wife of Fehrson, had guessed the treachery of her husband, for she had seen him ride past his own house as he came from Magno Wilson, and take the road which led to the officer's dwelling. Touched with pity, she warned Gustavus of his danger, and kindly provided him with a horse and sledge, so that he might fly at once.

Gustavus was very thankful to avail himself of the means of escape, and was soon flitting over the snow in his sledge beneath the starry sky in search of another place of refuge. The next morning, when Arendt Fehrson arrived with his twenty men, he was told that his guest had been missing since the evening before, and that no one knew whither he was gone.

Gustavus at last reached the house of a true friend, a Swedish pastor, who helped him with good advice during the eight days he remained with him, and strengthened him in his resolve to arouse the Dalecarlians. But he dared not stay longer in this part of the country, because Arendt Fehrson had already spread the report of his being alive; and the pastor drove him to the village of Isale, where he was received into the cottage of an honest peasant named Swen Nilson, who did him good and faithful service.

One day when Gustavus was standing in the cottage, clad in his peasant's garb, which was beginning to be the worse for wear, a body of Danish soldiers employed to track the fugitive, rushed in, breathless and anxious, and asked if a young nobleman, a well known traitor to the king, were not concealed about the place. Nilson answered, No; and his wife, to remove suspicion, gave Gustavus a sharp blow with a long wooden spoon, and scolded him loudly for standing idle instead of going to work in the barn with the others. Gustavus took the hint, and hastened out of the cottage, thus escaping from his pursuers, who did not for one moment suppose that the general of the Swedish army, and the descendant of kings, was concealed beneath so humble a disguise.

Front. *Gustavus Vasa in the Swedish peasant's hut.*

After this Swen Nilson had the courage to drive his guest in a cart loaded with straw to Rättwik. It was a dangerous journey: the Danish soldiers guarded all the passes and bridges, and some of them plunged their weapons into the straw, and wounded Gustavus severely in the leg as he lay covered up at the bottom of the cart. He bore the pain in silence, but unfortunately the blood dripped from the wound through the cart, and would have betrayed the fact that he lay hidden there, had not Nilson thought of cutting open the heel of his horse, so that the blood appeared to be trickling from that. Happily the hurt was not dangerous, and the moment after it was bound up on his arrival at Rättwik, Gustavus went to the church, where a great crowd of people had assembled, and without making himself known, he told them of the horrible cruelty of the King of Denmark, and how Sweden would never be free unless they roused themselves, as their brave ancestors would have done, to shake off the shameful bondage.

The peasants listened in horror, they were moved by his words, and said they would take up arms as soon as they could find out how their neighbours were disposed in the matter. Gustavus thought he had gained something, and went on joyfully to Mora, the largest and most populous parish in the valley. The news of his coming got spread abroad, and the Danish governor, who dwelt in the strong castle of Westeras, began to tremble; he knew that the inhabitants of the valleys, if once aroused, could make themselves very terrible. So he doubled the heavy price already set upon the head of Gustavus, and told the people around that none of the deeds reported to be done at Stockholm had really been carried out, and that Christiern was a most kind and merciful sovereign!

It was Christmas-time when Gustavus arrived in Mora: the peasants had come down from their distant mountain homes to make merry with their friends in the valley, and one day he went up to the top of a hill, and spoke to a vast concourse of people, who had followed him out of curiosity. Here again some of the peasants were touched by his words; their eyes filled with tears, and they signified by their shouts and cheers that they were willing to aid him. But others were of a different mind; they did not want to go to war; the nobles had hitherto been chiefly the objects of the king's cruelty, and they thought that they should be left in peace themselves. They were very near fetching their weapons, and chasing the speaker by force from the spot. A turn of good fortune, however, came to Gustavus whilst he was still at Mora.

A party of a hundred Danes, having heard that he was there in the hope of rousing the peasants, rushed suddenly upon the place, making the air resound with their wild cries, and threatening to put every one they met to the sword if he were not given up. The peaceful people of Mora were unused to be thus disturbed, and they hastened to ring the church-bells, which were only rung when some great danger was at hand. The wind carried the sound of the bells to the neighbouring villages, and in a little while some thousand armed peasants were seen pouring into Mora. They stormed the great walled-in court around the pastor's house, where the Danes (alarmed in their turn) had taken refuge, broke down its gates with heavy wooden stakes, and only spared the lives of the soldiers on condition that they should not attempt to lay hands on Gustavus. This was the first time that arms had been taken up in his cause: it was a feeling of honour that prompted the Dalecarlian peasants to defend him, because they said that they should have been ashamed if any one demanding their help had been taken by force from amongst them.

Gustavus, thankful to his preservers, now quitted Mora, and took his way towards the western valleys, so that he might conceal himself in the wilder parts of the country, if the fury of his pursuers increased. Many Swedish nobles had already fled thither, and they came out of their hiding-places, and met together in the valley. And there came to Mora an old man named Lars Olosson, who had always been faithful to his country, and another brave man came from the forest, and entreated the people to take up arms. The peasants now saw that they were in earnest, and they hastened to seek for Gustavus, fearing that he might already have passed the boundary and entered Norway. But Swedish messengers can go on their errands very quickly, because all through their nine months of dreary winter the peasants wear long sliding-shoes, which enable them to flit over the snow with almost the speed of an arrow. These shoes are very strange looking things; they are long, narrow pieces of fir-wood, the one worn on the right foot being three feet in length, and that on the left foot seven. The messengers found Gustavus in a parish called Lima, and he was joyful indeed when he came back to Mora, and saw that two hundred peasants were ready to follow him at once. Their numbers soon increased, and he divided them into little companies, which had their headquarters, so that they could all fight in unity: they were hardy, long-lived men, and could be quite content to live upon coarse meal stirred in water, or a little bread made of the bark of the trees if they could get no better food. And Gustavus still went up the steep mountain paths from cottage to cottage, and from one country house to another to try and persuade the people to help him, and before the ice had melted on the rivers and lakes the number of his followers had increased to several thousand. He chose sixteen of the youngest and bravest for his bodyguard, and maintained strict discipline amongst his men, although he was greatly beloved by them for his kindness of heart.

The first attempt they made was on the strong castle of the Governor of the Koppar Mountain, which they captured, together with the stores of provisions it contained. Amongst these was a large chest full of money, which Gustavus divided amongst his followers, and another day they captured some pieces of silk, which they made into banners, but they had neither powder nor balls as yet.

Now that Gustavus had so large an army he wanted to begin the war by a bold stroke, and he drew off towards Westeras, the governor of the strong fortress there, being at the time absent in Stockholm. Here he gained a great victory over the Danes, which prepared the way to future success, but the manner in which a great part of his army rejoiced over the triumph they had won, was not at all to his taste. It happened thus: some of his troops had gone on in advance, and after a desperate struggle got possession of the place, whilst Gustavus was still in the forest with the rear of his army. After the affray they found some huge casks of wine and brandy, which they carried off to the Council House, and foolishly regaled themselves with until they all fell to quarrelling, or were heavy with sleep. The greatest disorder prevailed; the Danes took advantage of the tumult to renew the attack; and would have recovered the fortress had not Gustavus appeared with the rest of the army. He was very angry indeed with his men, and had to fight hard to drive back the Danes, so that a great number of soldiers were killed on either side; and when the battle was over he caused the hoops to be removed from the casks of wine that remained, and let it all flow away on the ground in sight of his whole army. This was in the month of May in the year 1521, when the short Swedish spring was changing to summer, and the land, having cast off its mantle of snow, looked fresh, and green, and full of hope. In the northern climes the flowers bloom, and the leaves come back to the trees very quickly, and a few weeks sunshine is sufficient to ripen the barley and the rye, or the corn, in the places where it will grow.

After the battle of Westeras the peasants armed themselves in the plains of Sweden; the nobles headed them, and many officers deserted from the Viceroy whom King Christiern had left in Stockholm to manage the affairs of the State. The Viceroy and Trolle were friends; they soon began to be greatly alarmed; but they could get no succour from Denmark because the people there disliked them so much, and were getting so tired of the evil doings of their king. Many battles were fought, and the Swedes were not always successful, but at last Gustavus got possession of Stockholm after having besieged it three times; and a happy day came, when he entered the capital surrounded by senators, officers, and the first nobles in the land, and repaired to the great church, where—kneeling at the foot of the altar,—he thanked the Almighty aloud, for having preserved him through so many dangers, and granted him success. And then he went to the palace, where he wept for those whom he had loved very dearly, and now missed on this day of his triumph. Not only had his father and his brother-in-law perished in the massacre at Stockholm, but his mother Cecilia, and two of his sisters, had been cruelly put to death during the siege. It is said that if the siege had been raised their lives would have been spared, but these brave women knew in that case their country would have been lost, and they were content to die for its sake.

In the year 1523 the Danes would not have Christiern to reign over them any longer, and made his uncle Frederic, Duke of Holstein, king in his stead. Christiern was forced to leave the country, and retired into Flanders, with his wife and children. When Sigbritt had to leave the royal palace, she did not dare venture out of it, even in disguise, and was carried to the vessel destined to receive her concealed in a large chest.

The Swedes, full of gratitude and love for their preserver, wanted him to be crowned King of Sweden. Gustavus, however, refused this honour, and governed the country for some time as administrator. But as the years went on and it was in danger from the plots made by the Roman Catholics and the friends of Christiern, he yielded to the wishes of the people, and in June, 1527, was solemnly crowned King of Sweden under the title of Gustavus the First. He had long forgiven all the offences that had been offered him, whilst he remembered every little act of kindness that had been shown him when he was wandering about, a wretched fugitive, in hourly danger of his life. During the thirty-three years he reigned his great care was to make his subjects happy, and he was fully employed in setting his country in order, after the misery it had suffered for so many years. It was Gustavus who settled the Protestant faith throughout the land, and Luther, and Melancthon, and other great Protestant divines, used frequently to visit his court. He wished to inspire his people with a taste for arts and sciences, and encouraged learning by inviting studious and clever men to Stockholm: printing had been already introduced into Sweden about the year 1483, when Sten Sture the Elder founded the famous School or University at Stockholm. The king employed his peasants in working fresh mines and salt springs; he caused hops to be grown in Sweden, so that the iron sent out yearly in exchange for that produce might be kept in the country, and prove the source of comfort and wealth. Any merchant or tradesman convicted of dishonesty was punished with extreme rigour, and the bad laws were done away with, and good ones ordained in their place. The palace was open to all who demanded audience, when the king was ever ready to hear complaints, or to give advice. He thought the Bible the best of all books, and grounded his actions on its holy precepts; and the Swedes were so happy under his just and merciful rule that they always cried when he went abroad, "Long live Gustavus, the best loved of kings!" Soon after he came to the throne he married Catherine, daughter of the Duke of Magnus, whose sister had just espoused the Crown Prince of Denmark. Catherine died young, and Gustavus next married Margaret, daughter of an ancient senator, the Governor of East Gothnia: this lady was amiable and beautiful, and made her husband and her children very happy. The king used to tell his children not to be proud of their high estate, saying, "One man is as good as another, and when the play is over we are all equal;" meaning, when the life of trial upon earth was ended. The only approach to vanity in his character was to be seen in his love for magnificent apparel; but this was quite an excusable fault, when it is remembered how content he was to wear the coarse peasant's dress in the days of his misfortunes.

At the last assembly he convoked at Stockholm in the year 1560, he was led into the Senate House, where his four sons, Erick, John, Magnus, and Charles, and all the orders in the kingdom were assembled. He then caused his will to be read, and made his children swear to obey it. Erick was declared successor to the throne; John, possessor of Finland; Magnus of Eastern Gothnia; and Charles of Sudermania. In a few earnest words he urged his people to obey his successor and to preserve the greatest unity among themselves; since on that would depend their strength and their freedom: he said also, that if he had ever done any good, thanks for it were to be ascribed to God alone, and implored pardon for all the faults he had committed.

Very soon after this he died, leaving a name which is still cherished in the heart of every Swede; for he was called not only the king, but the father and the instructor of his people. It must not be thought that his long reign was free from care, since he had constantly to preserve himself from the attempts that were made by the friends of Christiern to take his power from him.

When he came to the throne he found the country laid waste by the ravages of war, and its people almost without hope. He left Sweden free and happy, an army ready to march at a moment's notice, and a treasury full of money; indeed, it is said, that after his death a great vaulted chamber was found so full of silver that the door of it could scarcely be opened.

Gustavus never forgot that he owed his success to the brave Dalecarlians; and his watch word, when about to engage on any expedition attended with danger, was always, "God and the Swedish peasants!"

BERTRAND DU GUESCLIN,

THE HERO OF CHIVALRY.

About the year 1320 Bertrand du Guesclin was born in the castle of La Motte Bron, which stood in a picturesque part of Bretagne, about six leagues from the city of Rennes. His father, Reynauld du Guesclin, was a brave and loyal knight, who served God truly, and was very kind to the poor, giving them a great part of his substance, although he was not at all rich himself.

Bertrand was the eldest of ten children. Unhappily his excessive ugliness made him an object of dislike to his mother, and she was not nearly so kind to him as she was to her other children. Besides this, he was self-willed and savage, and his temper would break out into fits of violence which terrified his little brothers and sisters, and exposed him to the contempt of the whole household. This rough and repelling exterior, however, only hid for a time a generous nature and a feeling heart, and many were the tears poor Bertrand shed in solitude, for he was too proud to let them be seen, when he rebelled against the harsh treatment he received on account of his ill-behaviour.

One day the lady of La Motte was seated at table in the dining-hall of the castle with her younger sons, Guillaume and Olivier, whilst Bertrand was eating his dinner in a corner apart. It was very sad to know that the eldest son of the family behaved so rudely that his parents would not allow him to take his place at the table. But this day it happened that some chance word of ridicule reached him in his corner, and he arose in fury, and, rushing towards the table, commanded his brothers to make room for him at the upper end, where his place as the eldest child should have been by right. His brothers, surprised at the tone of his voice, obeyed, and his mother suffered him to sit in the highest place; but he had not been there long before his awkward and uncouth manners obliged her to order him to return to his corner. Bertrand arose, and in his rage clenched his hand, and hit the oaken table so hard a blow that it overturned, and emptied the contents of the dishes into the laps of the persons seated around it. This passionate act of course called down a fresh torrent of reproaches on his head. In the midst of all the disorder a lady, who was a frequent visitor at the castle, entered the hall. She asked Bertrand's mother why she was so angry. The lady of

La Motte answered her by pointing to her little son, who was now sobbing bitterly in his corner. The lady went up to him, and although he was sullen at first, she soon persuaded him to tell her his sorrows. She invited him to return to the table, and Bertrand, to the astonishment of all who were present, took the dish of peacock which the steward was just bringing into the hall, and a goblet of wine, and served her with them himself, awkwardly it must be confessed, but in a spirit of gratitude for the few kind words she had spoken.

The lady who had thus befriended him was the daughter of a Jewish physician, but with her father had been converted to Christianity. She was reputed to be very clever, and was skilled in an art which was much practised in those days, namely, that of foretelling future events by observing the lines in people's hands, very much in the same manner as gipsies pretend to tell fortunes, even in our own time. After dinner she called Bertrand to her, and attentively examined his face and his hand, and presently told his mother that she ought to be proud of having such a son, instead of despising him, because she was convinced that when he grew up to be a man he would do great things for the glory of his country. From this day his mother looked more kindly upon him; she had him dressed for the first time in a manner suitable to his rank, and commanded the servants to treat him with the respect due to the eldest son of their master.

Bertrand's fiery temper, however, and his love of fighting, were a continual source of trouble and anxiety to his parents. Before he was nine years of age he would often leave the castle without their knowledge, and collect all the children he met with on his way, and then fight them one by one, or try his strength against a number of them together. When he returned home, bleeding, and with torn and soiled garments, his mother would justly reprove him for behaving so little like a gentleman.

At last his fighting propensities increased to such a pitch that the country people complained of him to his father, and the Sire de la Motte was obliged to order a forfeit to be paid by the parents of all children who were found in his company. Nevertheless Bertrand still contrived to get out of the castle secretly, and to lead the little villagers to their mimic battles. His father, as a last resource, shut him up in the dungeon of the castle, and in this dreary place he remained four months. But one evening a maid-servant, whose office it was to bring him his food twice a day, left the door open behind her, and Bertrand managed to slip out, not forgetting in his haste to turn the key upon her, in case she should betray him to his parents. Then he ran as fast as ever he could to a field, unfastened a mare from one of his father's ploughs, mounted it, laughing heartily the while at the ploughman, who was rushing after him, and galloped as far as Rennes, without saddle or bridle, to the house of his aunt, a sister of the Sire de la Motte, who was married to a knight of great honour.

His aunt had often heard of his misconduct at home, and was not at all pleased to see him arrive in such plight. She began scolding him in harsh words, when luckily for him his uncle intervened in his favour, reminding his wife that Bertrand was only a child, and had done nothing yet to forfeit his honour. "He is brave and spirited," said the good knight; "let us keep him in our house, and see if we cannot transform him into a great captain for the glory of Bretagne."

Bertrand remained with his uncle at Rennes until he was sixteen, and learned from him all the accomplishments necessary for a knight. Moreover, he learned to be gentle and courteous to those around him, and in these happier circumstances the good points of his character shone forth, and his violent temper was curbed, whilst his spirit remained free. It is related of him that he was so generous, that when he met with any poor persons, and had no money with him, he would give them some of the very clothes he wore, and if he had only a penny would share it with those who were in need. He found his greatest delight in listening to his uncle's stories of battles and sieges, and when some noble exploit was related, would clap his hands for joy, whilst his eyes shone like fire.

A very great fault, however, still remained to him, and that was his love of fighting. One Sunday it was announced in the city of Rennes that a prize would be given to the youth who should acquit himself best in single combat. Bertrand burned with impatience to enter the lists, and his aunt, fearing the temptation might prove too strong for him, carried him off with her to church, thinking he would certainly be safe there under her vigilant eye. As soon as Bertrand saw that her attention was fully absorbed in listening to the sermon, he took the opportunity of slipping out of church, and ran at full speed to the market-place. Here he was recognised by some of his opponents of former years, but he made them promise not to betray him to his aunt, and was just going to enter the lists, when a young Breton, who had thrown twelve of his competitors to the ground, advanced proudly to claim the prize, which was a hat with feather and silver band.

Bertrand defied him to the combat, and after a long struggle succeeded in overthrowing him; but during the time he had happened to fall on his opponent, and in so doing had cut his knee severely with a stone. This accident caused him so much pain that he could hardly stand, and he begged his comrades to take him to a surgeon's, where his wound could be dressed. The prize was brought to him there, but he dared not accept it, for fear his aunt, of whom he always seems to have had a wholesome dread, should hear of what he had done. She had indeed missed him, and had sought for him everywhere, and she did not spare her reproaches when she discovered the state he was in. Nevertheless she showed him greater kindness than he deserved, and nursed him until he had recovered from his wound.

The knight at last persuaded his father to recall him to the castle of La Motte Bron. Now Bertrand tasted the real joy of home for the first time, for his father was so delighted at the improvement in his character that he no longer withheld his love from him, and every member of the household had a kind word for him; while in former times, when he was so very naughty and unruly, there had only been complaints and reproofs.

The Sire Du Guesclin took care that the martial studies of his son should be completed, and gave him a little horse, on which Bertrand rode about to visit the great lords in the neighbourhood, and was present at the jousts and tournaments which were so often held at that time. Du Guesclin's poverty and youth prevented him, however, from entering the lists, and making known his courage and martial skill to the world. He grieved, too, because he was so ugly, and so humbly equipped, his famed steed being "little better than a miller's horse."

The time came at last when he was enabled to distinguish himself. A great tournament was announced at Rennes on the marriage of Jeanne de Penthièvre, heiress to the duchy of Bretagne, with Charles de Blois, who was nephew to the King of France. The Sire de la Motte Bron judged it to be a fit occasion for the display of his dignity, and went with the nobles of Bretagne to Rennes, followed by a great number of his vassals; whilst poor Bertrand, mounted on his insignificant horse, and easily recognised by the roundness and largeness of his head, his short nose, his strongly-marked eyebrows, and his square-set figure, was an object of ridicule to the peasants as they flocked along the road to Rennes. The tournament used to be held in an open space inside the city, and the ladies, richly attired, looked on from the windows and balconies around.

Bertrand's eyes flashed when he reached the arena where the knights were already engaged, and heard the sound of the trumpets and the clashing of the weapons. "I shall never please the ladies," he said, as he had said many a time before, "but I will make my name to be feared by the enemies of my country."

Seeing one of his relations retire from the combat, he followed him to his house, and, throwing himself on his knees before him, implored him to lend him some armour and a horse. His cousin good-naturedly lent him a fresh horse, and armed him himself, and Bertrand rushed back to the tournament, and, having entered the lists without naming himself, challenged a knight, and quickly overthrew him. Another knight now came forward to avenge the vanquished one, and Bertrand was just going to attack him, when he saw his father's arms upon his shield, and bowing low, withdrew, to the astonishment of the spectators. After this he challenged no fewer than fifteen knights without coming to grief himself. All the people present were now very anxious to know his name, and one of the ladies who sat in the great balcony entreated a Norman knight to descend into the arena, and, if possible, remove the visor from the victor's face. The knight went down, and had just succeeded in removing the helmet from Bertrand's head, when a strong arm suddenly lifted him off his horse and laid him in the dust. Then Reynauld du Guesclin recognised his son, and hastened to embrace him in his pride and joy, and Bertrand was proclaimed victor over all to the sound of the trumpets, and received the prize, which was a beautiful silver swan, life size. The prize, however, he did not keep for himself, but gave it to his cousin, whose kindness had enabled him to win so great renown.

When Bertrand was twenty years of age he was no longer contented with displaying his prowess in tournaments, but began to fight in good earnest, taking the part of Charles de Blois in a quarrel that lasted for a very long time between that prince and his rival, Jean de Montfort.

Jean de Bretagne, known by the name of the Good Duke, had died without leaving any childhood, and was succeeded by his brother, Guy, Count of Penthièvre, whose daughter's marriage with Charles de Blois had occasioned the festivity at Rennes. Charles thus claimed the duchy in right of his wife; but Guy was no sooner dead than his half-brother, Jean de Montfort, came forward, and maintained that his title to Bretagne was a better one than that of his niece.

This was not true, because the right of female succession had been fully established in the duchy, and the King of France and many of the Breton nobles sided with Charles, while the King of England sent assistance to De Montfort.

The wives of both princes were women of extraordinary spirit. Jeanne, Countess de Montfort, defended her husband's rights whilst he lived, and after his death those of his son, who was likewise named Jean; and once during the war, when she was shut up in the town of Hennebon, she held out, like a brave and skilful general, against all the attacks of the enemy until Sir Walter Manny arrived with succour from King Edward the Third of England. Jeanne de Penthièvre was a woman of equal courage, but her pride and ambition caused her husband to risk the battle which cost him his life, and proved, as will be seen hereafter, the ruin of her own cause.

Du Guesclin chose the side of Charles de Blois because he believed it to be the right one. "Never," said he, "while I live, will I maintain an unrighteous cause." He was soon at the head of sixty men, in readiness to serve, and sold his mother's jewels that he might be able to buy horses, harness, and arms. His chroniclers tell us, however, how he very soon captured from an English knight, whom he met in a forest, a treasure consisting of jewels, which he gave to his mother in compensation for those she had lost. Although gunpowder was known in those days, it was very little used; the chief weapons were swords, lances, battle-axes, cross-bows, and clubs; and every warrior defended himself with the shield. Bertrand's name came to be feared by his enemies, as he had predicted in the days gone by: his first attempts in warfare were chiefly against the English, who held many of the fortresses in Bretagne for Jean de Montfort. A story is told of the manner in which he gained possession of one of these, the Castle of Fougeray, which was a very important place.

Bertrand knew all the ins and outs of the castle, because in the chances of war he had once been a prisoner for a short time within its walls, and he disguised himself, and about twenty of his companions in arms, as wood-cutters, in white gowns reaching down to the knee, and with bundles of faggots on their shoulders, as he had often seen the poor peasants bringing wood to the castle. He divided his men, to make it appear that they were coming from different parts of the country to sell their wood, and waited for the time when the governor should have gone out of his stronghold with a part of the garrison. When all was ready they passed the night securely in the forest, and came out of it in the grey dawn of the morning with their bundles on their shoulders.

The watchman of Fougeray saw them dimly in the distance, and rang the bell, to give the alarm, but all fear vanished when it was seen that only wood-cutters were coming towards the castle. Bertrand advanced to the drawbridge, and asked the porter if he did not want wood. The porter said that he did, and not suspecting any harm, let down the drawbridge at once. Du Guesclin laid down his heavy load of wood so as to prevent the bridge from being drawn up, and rushed on to the castle, shouting "Guesclin," the war cry which afterwards became so terrible to his enemies. His comrades followed quickly at his summons; the unhappy porter fell wounded in the struggle, and as there were a hundred men in the place and Bertrand had only sixty when all had come to his aid, the conflict was very sharp; women and children even throwing showers of stones on the heads of the Bretons. Du Guesclin himself was severely wounded, and was found defending himself to the last, without his hatchet, when a party of cavalry belonging to Charles de Blois came up in time to secure possession of the castle. The whole affair may have been considered an ingenious trick, but I think it would have been more noble for Bertrand to have ridden up openly to his enemies, clad in his armour, and with his sword in his hand, than to have deceived them by the woodcutter's guise.

The war went on, and at last the King of England sent Henry, the good Duke of Lancaster, to Bretagne at the head of a large force, with orders to lay siege to Rennes, the city where Bertrand had passed the happiest days of his boyhood, and which had twice been the scene of his triumphs. Besides all the great English nobles who had accompanied the duke, the army was increased by many Breton gentlemen who had enlisted themselves on the side of Jean de Montfort, and Lancaster made a solemn vow not to depart from Rennes until he had planted his standard upon its walls.

Bertrand concealed himself in a forest near the city, and constantly harassed his enemies by rushing suddenly upon them, by day and by night, and always to the cry of "Guesclin," until at last the Duke of Lancaster swore that if ever the brave Breton captain fell into his hands, he would never let him free, however large a ransom might be offered for him.

Lancaster made several attempts upon Rennes, but with little success. One day an English officer who had been captured by Du Guesclin, told him that his countrymen intended to undermine the city and open a breach. Upon this news Bertrand contrived one very dark night to glide with his Bretons into the midst of the English camp, where all was silent, and set fire to some of the tents. The enemy, awakened by the usual cry of "Guesclin," thought that Charles de Blois had fallen upon them with his army, and were very angry as they put out their fires to find it was only Bertrand with his handful of men.

The governor of Rennes now gave orders that in all the houses near the ramparts little copper basins should be hung with one or two balls of brass in each, so that by the jingling of the metal, which the movement of the miners would cause, it might be known in what direction they were at work. By this means the garrison were enabled to work against them until the mine was pierced, and the besiegers found a body of troops ready to beat them back.

The Duke of Lancaster now thought of another plan for subduing the people of Rennes. Knowing that they were almost without provisions, he caused two thousand pigs to be assembled in a field near the walls of the city, hoping that the hungry inhabitants would come out for the purpose of capturing them. The governor, however, was not to be outwitted, and had a sow attached by a rope to the gate of Rennes, with its head downwards. The sow struggled so hard to free itself and grunted and squeaked so loud that the other pigs were naturally attracted to the spot. When the besieged saw that the pigs were coming in that direction they lowered the drawbridge, and cut the rope. The sow, thus released, ran joyfully back into the city, followed by all the other pigs, and it was certain that the famished people of Rennes had a good meal that day and for many days after.

Du Guesclin performed numerous acts of daring during the siege, and one day, when the Bretons had eaten up the two thousand pigs and were very near dying of hunger again, he intercepted and captured a hundred waggons, loaded with wine, flour, and salt meat, which were on their way to the English camp; but when he found that the waggoners were supplying these provisions to the enemy at their own cost, he paid them liberally for all that he had seized.

The Duke of Lancaster now prepared a huge machine which was often used in those times of warfare. This was a wooden tower on wheels, as high as the walls of the city, which contained a number of men inside, who shot surely from it with their arrows. The tower would have caused great havoc, had not Bertrand one night crawled out with his Bretons, and completely destroyed it by fire.

Winter was now coming on: the lengthened siege had lost the lives of many brave men, and Henry of Lancaster at last sent a herald to Du Guesclin to tell him that he desired to speak with him. The herald brought a written passport which, alas! Bertrand was obliged to have read to him by one of his comrades. He had always been so heedless and disobedient in the old days at La Motte, that no one had been able to teach him to read or write, and he had never succeeded in learning in after years, although some authors assert that he could really sign his name.

Bertrand dismissed the herald with a handsome present of clothes and money, and then repaired to the camp of the brave English duke. When there he was asked by Lancaster, whom he owned for his master. "Charles de Blois," he replied promptly, "to whom Bretagne belongs in right of his wife."

The Duke was much pleased with his boldness and resolution, and offered him a high rank in his army if he would consent to enter his service; but Bertrand replied that nothing should ever shake him in his fidelity to Charles de Blois.

Lancaster now received orders from his father to raise the siege: yet he could not depart, in remembrance of the oath he had taken, and Du Guesclin proposed that he should enter the city with ten of his knights, and plant his standard on its walls. When this was done, Du Guesclin politely asked him where the war was to be carried on in future. "Bertrand, my fair friend," replied the duke, "you shall soon know." He had scarcely gone past the barrier when he saw his standard thrown down into the moat; nevertheless he had kept his oath, and having raised the siege, he decamped with all his host, and went to pass the winter at Auray.

Du Guesclin was quick to resent an affront offered to any member of his family. The Duke of Lancaster with the brave Sir John Chandos was before Dinan, which town Bertrand, his brother Olivier, and the governor who had defended Rennes, had hastened to enter before the enemy could invest it. One day when all was quiet, Olivier Du Guesclin had gone out of the town unarmed for the purpose of amusing himself in the open country, when he met with an English knight, who asked him his name, and behaved in a very haughty manner towards him, and made him walk on first, vowing that he should not escape until he had given him a thousand good florins. A Breton knight, however, who had seen Olivier made prisoner, hastened to tell Du Guesclin what had happened. Bertrand instantly mounted his horse and rode off to the English camp, where he found the Duke of Lancaster in his tent playing at chess with Sir John Chandos, whilst several of the chief nobles were standing around looking on. They were all glad to see Bertrand because they had a great respect for his valour, and it is true that he had many qualities which endeared him to his fellow-men, and gained for him friendships which lasted as long as life.

Du Guesclin would not drink the wine they poured out for him until justice had been done to his brother. Henry of Lancaster was an upright man, and promised to settle the matter fairly. He summoned the offending knight to his presence, and ordered him to release Olivier at once. But the knight, who was called Thomas of Canterbury, would not allow that the complaint made against him by Bertrand was just, and threw down his iron glove in defiance. It was soon known in Dinan that a terrible combat would take place between the two knights, and the people feared that Du Guesclin would fall, because the Englishman was possessed of such extraordinary strength and skill. But a very beautiful young lady of noble family in Dinan, named Tiphaine de Raguenel, whom Bertrand married soon after the siege was raised, predicted that he would triumph over his foe. Tiphaine was called an astrologer, because she professed to foretell by observing the stars in the heavens, whether people were to be prosperous in their lives or unfortunate; happy or miserable. This was very foolish, and we know better in our own times than to put faith in such a science; and even in Dinan, when by chance Tiphaine's predictions came true, the people looked upon her with distrust and called her a witch. The Duke of Lancaster with all his nobles came into the town to witness the combat, which ended to the great joy of the inhabitants of Dinan in the triumph of Bertrand, and the offending knight was ordered by Lancaster to retire from his service.

The siege of Dinan was raised by our King Edward, who had King John of France at this time a prisoner in the palace of the Savoy. Du Guesclin went on fighting for Charles de Blois, until at last the younger Jean de Montfort got weary of the war, and proposed to his rival that the Duchy of Bretagne should be halved between them; and that Rennes should be the capital of Charles's dominions, and Nantes the capital of his own. Charles de Blois was a man who loved peace; he agreed solemnly to divide the duchy as Jean had proposed, and would have kept faith with him, had not his wife broken out into a violent passion as soon as she heard what he had done, and overruled him by saying that she would never consent to so shameful a settlement, and that she had married him to defend the whole of her duchy, and not the half of it. The war must have broken out again at once if the good offices of Lancaster had not effected a truce for a time.

When King John came back to France he invited Du Guesclin to enter his service, and gave him the command of a hundred lances. Each lance, or man-at-arms, was attended by three archers, a man armed with a cutlass, and a page, so that a company of a hundred lances really included six hundred men. Du Guesclin had the permission to form his troop of the gentlemen of Bretagne, of whom many were his relations and friends; and with these he set out hopefully to take part in a war which King John was carrying on in Normandy against the wicked King of Navarre.

Bertrand did the king good service in Normandy, and captured the towns of Mantes and Meulan. At the latter place he lost all patience with the tardiness of the besiegers, and seizing a ladder, began to mount it with his sword in his hand, and his shield on his breast. He was just mounting the last steps and boasting to the Baron of Mereuil who was on the other side of the wall, that he would soon make him feel the strength of his arm, when the baron threw some heavy stones on the ladder, which dashed it to pieces, and Bertrand fell with his head downwards into the ditch around the city wall. The ditch was full of water, and Bertrand was taken out by his comrades half dead, but he scarcely waited for his injuries to be healed, before he began to fight with greater vigour than before, and a little while later gained the battle of Cocherel over the Captal de Buche, who was fighting for the King of Navarre, and took the Captal prisoner.

King John was now dead, and Charles the Wise was on the throne of France. The victory at Cocherel had served to raise the spirits of the French, who had been much cast down by their defeats during the two last sieges, and the fame of Du Guesclin was spoken all over the country.

But the war unhappily broke out in Bretagne once more. Jean de Montfort, angry with his rival for his breach of faith, came with his army to invest the town of Auray. The people there were in great need and misery, and lighted fires every night on the summits of their towers in token of their distress. Charles de Blois set off at once to assist them in their danger, but his wife at parting, charged him on no account whatever to agree to any division of the duchy. Du Guesclin and many brave nobles and knights hastened to join his army; and when they arrived in sight of Auray, De Montfort sent a herald to them to propose peace on the terms that had already been made, or to demand an immediate battle.

Charles de Blois, weakly dreading the anger of his wife if he gave way, sent the herald back without an answer, although in his heart he was longing more than ever to be at peace.

In the disastrous battle of Auray which began soon after, and lasted for seven hours, Charles de Blois lost his life, the celebrated Oliver Du Clisson an eye, and Du Guesclin his liberty. It was late in the day, and Bertrand was left almost alone upon the battle field with the dead lying around him; he had been thrown from his horse, and surrounded by his enemies, but he had risen from the ground and defended himself single-handed to the last. Now the blood was flowing from his wounds; his sword was broken; the handle had been wrenched off his battle-axe, and Sir John Chandos found him armed only with an iron hammer. It was useless for him to resist longer, and when he had given up the broken piece of his sword into the hands of the English knight, the battle was at an end.

Charles de Blois had fought that day like one in despair. With his last breath he had said that he had long waged war against his conscience. And thus the feud was ended which had lasted for nearly twenty years; Jean de Montfort could have the whole duchy of Bretagne for himself, and the unhappy widow of his rival had the sorrow of remembering that it was her own pride and unbending spirit which had cost her the life of her husband. The people of Bretagne were so tired of war that when, a little while after, the treaty, which Jean de Montfort was making with Jeanne, could not be settled, they assembled in a vast concourse and throwing themselves on the ground, implored the Count to give them peace.

The King of France did not suffer Bertrand to remain a captive long. The country was at that time infested by bands of lawless men of various nations, who called themselves "Free Companies," and used to go about laying waste the orchards and fields, sacking and burning the castles of the nobility; and making war just as they pleased. The greater number of these men were disbanded soldiers, whose services were no longer needed now that the war was at an end.

Their power became very formidable when such men as Sir Hugh de Caverlay, the Green Knight, Sir Matthew Gournay, and many others who were renowned for their valour, joined them, and elected themselves their leaders.

The thought occurred to King Charles that Du Guesclin was the one man capable of ridding his country of so terrible a scourge, and he hastened to pay the hundred thousand francs which his enemies had required for his ransom, and told him that if he would consent to drive the Free Companies out of France, he might choose his own method of carrying out his purpose.

Du Guesclin went to the camp where the Free Lances were assembled, and, as many of the leaders had already served under his banner, he found little difficulty in persuading them to go with him into Spain on a crusade against the Saracens, who still retained possession of a part of that country. But a war had already broken out between Pedro the Second of Spain and his half brother, Henry of Trastamare. Pedro had made himself hateful to his subjects by repeated acts of tyranny, and worst of all had suffered his wife, Blanche de Bourbon, to be cruelly murdered. This princess was very amiable and lovely; she was sister to the Queen of France, and granddaughter to the good Saint Louis, and Charles, indignant and sorrowful at her unhappy fate, thought the services of Du Guesclin would be better employed in driving Pedro from the throne than in making war on the Saracens.

Bertrand was therefore ordered to hasten to the assistance of Henry of Trastamare, and one day he collected all the Free Companies at a place called Chalons sur Saone, and marched from thence southwards, to the great delight of the French nation, taking Avignon on his way, where the Pope then resided, instead of at Rome.

The companies went to Avignon to ask for absolution, because they had been excommunicated, that is to say, cut off from all fellowship with the church, on account of their lawless deeds. The Pope readily granted them absolution, but he was not nearly so ready to give them a large sum of money—which they asked for in addition to the 200,000 gold florins which they had already received from Du Guesclin—and it was only after a long delay, that he could be persuaded to give them any money at all.

The troops Du Guesclin led himself were called "The White Company," because they all wore a white cross on their shoulder, as a sign that they meant to abolish the religion of the Jews, which Pedro was supposed to favour. Pedro was very much alarmed at the approach of so vast an army; he happened to be engaged at the time in laying waste with fire and sword the lands belonging to his brother, whilst Henry himself was hiding in a castle with his wife and children, and for a long while could not be made to believe that the French hero was really coming to his aid.

Du Guesclin soon enabled him, however, to gain possession of several cities, and at a frontier town, called Maguelon Home, he took the title of King. And when the people of Burgos (which was the Christian capital of Spain at that time) heard of the approach of the White Company, they brought the keys of the city, and laid them at the feet of Henry, and joyfully acknowledged that he was King over Castille. Henry made a triumphant entry into Burgos, with Bertrand, his deliverer, clad in complete armour by his side; they went to the palace, where a great banquet was served before them, with the richest viands, while the whole city was one scene of rejoicing and merriment, and wine flowed in the streets like water; the people were so glad to be freed from the tyranny of Pedro the Second.

Bertrand having thus placed Henry of Trastamare on the throne, urged him to send for his wife Jeanne, that they might both be crowned the same day. And when the Queen was seen approaching the capital, Bertrand went out to meet her, accompanied by the bravest of his knights. As soon as the

Queen perceived that it was Du Guesclin who was advancing towards her, she alighted from her mule that she might render him the greater honour, and turning to his whole company, she exclaimed, "Friends, and gentlemen, it may truly be said that we hold the crown of Castille through you alone." Henry and Jeanne were crowned at Burgos on Easter-day of the year 1366, and the King, in gratitude for the services of Du Guesclin, gave him the Duchy of Molina, and made him constable of Castille.

Pedro meanwhile was in great terror at the approach of his brother, and kept himself concealed with his treasures in a forest a hundred leagues long. One of his treasures was a table of pure gold, inlaid with jewels, and engraven with the portraits of Charlemagne's twelve peerless knights. Amongst the gems was a carbuncle, which is said to have had the peculiar property of shining by night as brightly as the sun shines by day; and one very dark night, when Pedro was outside the walls of a city, and beset with dangers on every side, he was obliged to have his table fetched out from among his treasures, that he might discover by its light the means of escape. The stone may have possessed a singular brilliancy, but for the fact of its shining as brightly as the sunlight, I cannot vouch. It was said to have another strange property, that of changing colour and turning black directly poison approached it.

The forest was near the town of Cardonna, where Pedro had taken refuge, immediately after the great city of Toledo had surrendered to his brother. Henry supposed him to be still in the town, and went in pursuit of him with Du Guesclin, Hugh de Caverlay, Olivier de Mauny, and many other valiant men. Their way between Toledo and Cardonna lay through the long forest, which was full of wild beasts and snakes, and had neither villages nor houses of any kind in its depths. They were in this wild tract seven days, and lost many of their men there; some of them being devoured by the wild beasts, and others dying from the bites of the snakes. When they got to Cardonna they found, of course, that Pedro had fled, but they took possession of the town.

Now that Henry had really been placed on the throne, Bertrand thought he might carry out his original plan, and proceed to Granada, which was the stronghold and capital of the Moors in Spain. The Queen, however, with many tears implored him not to forsake her husband; she dreaded so much the anger and cruelty of Pedro, when he should come out of his hiding-place. And Pedro soon made himself dreaded once more, for he had found his way to Guienne and entreated the Black Prince, who held his court in that province, to protect him, and assist him with troops; and had offered him his golden table, and part of his treasures as an equivalent for his aid; promising him, besides, a large sum of money to defray the cost of an army. The Black Prince, either out of compassion for the fallen King, or because he did not like to see his rival in league with France, agreed to assist him; and in the spring of the year 1367 crossed the province of Navarre with Pedro, and a large army of Gascons, Normans, and English, and entered Castille.

The fortunes of Henry already began to decline: several of the Companies withdrew from his service, and enlisted themselves in preference under the banner of the Black Prince. Du Guesclin urged the King not to risk a decisive battle too soon, but he would not listen to him, and the two armies met at Najara, on the right bank of the river Ebro. The watchword of the Black Prince's army was "Guienne and St. George!" and that of King Henry's, "Castille and St. James!"

The battle proved disastrous for the King of Castille, his cavalry were forced to give way, and the rout becoming general he escaped from the field with very few of his followers. When Bertrand saw the King's discomfiture, he stationed himself against a wall, and with a battle-axe defended himself so vigorously that several Englishmen were overthrown by him; and at last his enemies dared not approach him, but only hurled at him their daggers and swords. The Black Prince, hearing of this, desired to see him, and went with his standard unfurled to the place where he stood. Bertrand recognised the Prince, and kneeling on one knee before him said, "To you, Sire, the Prince of Wales, I surrender myself and to no other; for I will never be the captive of Pedro, e'en though I die in my defence!"

The Prince received the submission of Du Guesclin graciously, and confided him to the keeping of the Captal de Buche, who in remembrance of his own capture by Bertrand in the battle of Cocherel, told him kindly that he might live with him at large, if he would give him his word not to escape. Du Guesclin, much pleased with the confidence reposed in him, swore, like a true knight, that he would rather die than break his word.

For six months he remained with the English army, and during that time had no cause to complain of his treatment. But as soon as he arrived at Bordeaux, where the Black Prince held his splendid Court, he was shut up in the prison of Hâ. One morning whilst he was there, three pilgrims, who had arrived in Bordeaux the evening before, had gone to hear mass in the Church of Notre Dame. One of these pilgrims was Henry of Trastamare, who had disguised himself thus in the hope of journeying safely to the Duke of Anjou, to entreat him to support his cause.

Several knights happened to be in the church, who had fought with Du Guesclin in the battle of Najara; they began talking of their common misfortunes, and Henry, taking one of them apart, asked news of Bertrand, and learned with sorrow that the Black Prince had made a vow never to ransom him or set him free. Henry went home with the knight to whom he had spoken, and told him who he was, and persuaded him to procure him the means of seeing Du Guesclin. So the knight concealed the King in his house, and went to the prison of Hâ, and told the gaoler that he was going to Bretagne to seek for money to pay his ransom, and that he greatly desired to see Du Guesclin before he started.

The gaoler did not admit him at once, but only hinted that such things were not done without a bribe. The knight assured him that Du Guesclin was most liberal, and would amply reward him if he would procure the interview. The gaoler owned that he was so proud of his prisoner, that he hoped such a man might never go out of his hands, and after a little more delay he conducted the knight to Bertrand, who thought that his visitor had come to borrow money, and was much surprised to hear that Henry of Trastamare was in Bordeaux in the disguise of a pilgrim of St. James. He called the gaoler, and told him that there was a poor pilgrim in the city, a native of Bretagne, and one of his own vassals, whom he wished to assist with money to enable him to complete his journey; and he begged him to take his seal and go to a certain Italian jew in the city, and ask him for the sum of 400 florins. The gaoler fetched the money; Du Guesclin gave him a hundred florins for himself, and by noon the King was admitted into the prison. A more sumptuous dinner than was usually seen within its walls was served in his honour, and they lingered over it, talking of their misfortunes and of the King's project for seeking aid from the Duke of Anjou; Du Guesclin would not, however, on any account suffer him to ask the duke to pay his ransom. Whilst they were at dinner the gaoler began to feel the pricks of his conscience, and he took his wife apart, and told her that he suspected some treason was going on between the pilgrim and Du Guesclin against his master the Black Prince, and that he must acquaint him with the whole affair. The gaoler's wife whispered her husband's intentions to Bertrand, and the brave knight, with a dexterity similar to that he had employed, when as a boy he freed himself from the dungeon of La Motte, did not suffer his keeper to pass through the prison wicket, but dealt him so heavy a blow with a stick that the poor man fell on his knees: then taking the keys from his pocket, he opened the door to Henry, who quickly disappeared with his two companions and the knight who had accompanied him thus far. Bertrand closed the door upon them, and keeping the keys, came back to the gaoler and, after giving him a good beating, shut him up in a room by himself, as a warning that the transaction was not to be breathed beyond the prison walls.

The Duke of Anjou assisted Henry, and enabled him to enter Burgos a second time, whilst Pedro was obliged to fly from the throne he had re-ascended after the battle of Najara. Many of the knights who had been taken prisoners in that contest were now ransomed, but Du Guesclin, "the scourge of the English," as he was called, was deemed too formidable an enemy to be set at large; and he might have remained in prison until his dying day, had not some of the English nobles, who held his qualities in high esteem, remonstrated with their prince in his favour, and taunted him by saying that he only retained his prisoner through fear.

The Black Prince at last resolved to have an interview with his captive, and Du Guesclin, overjoyed at the prospect of obtaining his release, rose hastily at the prince's summons, and appeared before him in the soiled and coarse grey robe he wore in his prison, but which could not detract from the dignity of his bearing. He told the prince that he was indeed weary of his long confinement; "I have listened to the rats and mice long enough," he said, "and I would fain go where I can hear the birds sing once more."

The prince told him that he would set him free that very day without a ransom, if he would swear never again to bear arms against him for France; or against Pedro for Henry. These conditions Bertrand of course could not accept, and before the interview was ended he had spoken with so much honesty and candour, that the Black Prince could not but own the righteousness of his cause, and requested him to name his own ransom. Bertrand fixed it at 100,000 gold florins, and when the prince asked him why he named so large a sum, he declared his ransom should not be less than 70,000 florins, adding that although he was a poor knight, the Kings of France and Castille would assuredly pay that sum for him; and that if they did not that the Breton women would spin till they had gained the money for him.

He was now set at liberty on condition of obtaining his ransom. The people of Bordeaux flocked to see him when he came out of his prison, and the Princess of Wales, Joanna the Fair, journeyed expressly from Angoulême to Bordeaux that she might have the honour of entertaining him at a banquet, and presented him besides with 10,000 francs towards his ransom. Sir John Chandos and Hugh de Caverlay helped also to raise the sum required. Chandos was always his friend, although he fought on the opposite side; and it may be that these brave men esteemed one another the more for clinging to what each one believed to be the right.

Du Guesclin had hardly gone a league on his way homewards when he met a poor knight who was returning to his prison in Bordeaux on foot, in a very forlorn condition, because he was unable to pay his ransom. Bertrand not only gave him the money to pay it, but also enough to set him up in arms.

The knight told him that the Duke of Anjou was then besieging the town of Tarascon. Bertrand was bound in honour not to fight; but he could not resist going to Tarascon, to aid the duke with his advice, and made the besieged tremble at the very sound of his name. And there he was in the midst of all the danger, and the clashing of weapons, mounted on his horse, but with a peeled rod in his hand, instead of a sword, for his oath's sake!

When he reached his own estate in Bretagne, he begged his wife to give him her jewels, and all the valuable things she possessed; but she told him that a number of poor knights and squires, all taken at Najara, had come to her in great distress, and that she had given them all she could find in the castle. Bertrand was very glad that his wife had been so kind to the poor men, and had not sent them away empty handed. The sum for his ransom was raised amongst his relations and friends, and he had set out for Bordeaux, when he met ten poor knights, whose ransoms he could not resist paying; preferring to remain a captive himself rather than to know that so many others were languishing in prison, away from their homes, and all whom they loved.

When the Black Prince heard of Bertrand's generosity, he did not shut him up in a dungeon again, but let him go about the city as he pleased on his word of honour that he would not escape. A day came when mules were seen approaching Bordeaux loaded with 70,000 good gold florins which the kings of France and Castille and the Duke of Anjou had sent to purchase his liberty.

Du Guesclin, a free man once more, devoted himself entirely to the cause of Henry, and defeated Pedro in a great battle near Toledo, notwithstanding the help afforded the Spanish King by the Moors. The fortunes of Pedro now rapidly declined, the Black Prince not caring to aid him again, because he had not kept the promises he made before the battle of Najara.

After a battle fought near Montiel, [11] in the south of Spain, Pedro took refuge in the Castle of Montiel, in which there was only one way of going in or coming out, and before this entrance Le Bègue de Vilaines, who was fighting for Henry, stationed himself with his pennon. In this extremity it was arranged that Pedro should make his escape from the castle at midnight with twelve of his companions. It was a dark misty night, and when Pedro crept out of the castle, Le Bègue, who stood waiting for him with three hundred men, could not see him, but fancied he heard the sound of footsteps.

"Who art thou?" he cried, "Speak, or thou art a dead man." The first one addressed escaped in the darkness. The next who came, Le Bègue believed to be the king, and asked him who he was with the dagger held close to his breast. Then Pedro, seeing he had no chance of escape, cried "Bègue, Bègue, I am the King, Don Pedro, of Castille;" and surrendering himself to him he implored him to take him to some place where he should be beyond the reach of his half-brother.

Le Bègue took him to his own quarters, but he had not been there long before Henry of Trastamare and some of his followers entered the chamber where he was concealed; and in the furious struggle which ensued Pedro was slain by the hands of his brother. Thus died this unhappy king, whose many evil deeds gained for him the surname of "The Cruel;" but Henry was very wicked and cruel also to take his brother's life, and could not have been happy when he remembered Montiel, although he had now undisputed possession of the throne.

Du Guesclin was now at liberty to return to his own country. The King of Castille parted from him with great regret, and gave him some handsome presents in token of gratitude for the services he had rendered him. Du Guesclin on his return, was constantly employed in the war which broke out again between England and France, and regained many of the places which the English had taken from the French. The time came when King Charles thought that the wisest measure he could pursue would be to make Bertrand, Constable of France, which was the highest office in all the realm. Bertrand was unwilling to accept so great an honour, saying that there were many men more worthy of it than himself. Charles declared, however, that there was neither prince nor noble in the land who would not cheerfully obey the brave knight, and Du Guesclin was made Constable. From that time he was surrounded by all the dignity and splendour of the court, and always sat at the table with the king.

But certain it is when men have reached their highest estate, they are very often near a fall. Bertrand was again employed in Bretagne, when meeting with some reverses, he incurred the king's displeasure. Charles, having listened to some evil reports which were spread against him, did not scruple to express his discontent, and Bertrand took the matter so much to heart that he resigned his Constable's sword, and was only induced to resume his office when the king found out that the reports were untrue, and tried to atone to him for the mistake he had made. In the year 1380, Bertrand was sent to drive the English out of the south of France. He was very glad to go thither, because it always grieved him to make war on the people of his own province of Bretagne. After reducing some places of little importance, he went to help his friend Sancerre in the siege of the Castle of Randan, which was possessed by the English, and some Gascons, who were unfriendly to France. The Constable pressed the siege with vigour and vowed that he would never depart from the spot till the castle was taken. And he never did depart from thence alive, for he was seized with a violent fever, which in a short time proved fatal. The knowledge of his danger made the besiegers more anxious than ever to gain the fortress, and the garrison were obliged at last to agree to surrender on a certain day.

The Sire de Roos, the governor of the castle, having been informed of the dangerous condition of Du Guesclin, desired to render up the keys into his own hands; and when the appointed day had arrived, he came out of the gates, followed by all the garrison. It was summer time, and the rays of the setting sun shone on their unfurled banners, as they went to the tent, where the dying Constable lay. His knights were standing sorrowfully around him; they could not bear to think that he would never rise from his bed again, that his voice would never more cheer them on to victory. The English themselves shed tears at the mournful spectacle.

When Du Guesclin had prayed that his sins might be forgiven him, he entreated the nobles and knights to be faithful to their king, and not make war, which would cause the blood of peasants, and defenceless old men, and women and children to be shed; remembering with sorrow how heedlessly he had himself waged war in the days of his youth. Then dismissing them all except his friend Du Clisson, he asked for his constable's sword, and prayed him to deliver it into the hands of the king, and when they had bidden each other a last farewell, Du Clisson stood by him in tears and in silence until his spirit passed away.

So died Du Guesclin, the Hero of Chivalry, a man with many failings, but brave and generous beyond comparison, and ever faithful to his friends. Although the violence of his temper broke out at intervals all his life long, he could be kind and gentle. Queens and princesses esteemed him for his respectful courtesy, and we like to read, how, when the Black Prince summoned him to his presence, the stern warrior was found playing merrily with his gaoler's children, inside the dreary walls of his prison.

Some authors assert that the governor of the Castle of Randan only laid the keys on the coffin of Du Guesclin; but the most probable account is that he really gave them into his hands before he died.

Charles the Wise grieved sincerely for the loss the country had sustained, and ordered the remains of the Constable to be interred in the Church of Saint Denis with almost regal pomp.

Jeanne de Laval, the second wife of Du Guesclin, founded several religious houses, and instituted services in memory of her illustrious husband.

FOOTNOTES:

[11] The green knight fell in this battle.

CHRISTOPHER COLUMBUS

Christopher Columbo, or Columbus, was born in the city of Genoa, about the year 1436. His father, Domenico Columbo, earned the bread of his family by combing wool, which, however lowly it may be thought at the present time, was once a very honourable occupation, and was invented three hundred years after the birth of our Lord by Blaise, the good martyr-bishop of Armenia, who to this day is regarded as the patron of woolcombers.

Christopher had two brothers, Bartholomew, and Diego, and one sister; of the latter there is nothing particular recorded. The three brothers loved one another dearly. Bartholomew had a brave and ardent spirit, and was fond of an active life; in the troubles and dangers they shared in after years Christopher would call him "another self;" and he said not long before he died that his brothers had always been his best friends. Christopher as a child was quiet and thoughtful. He loved to stand on the shore of the beautiful bay spreading out at the feet of Genoa, "the city of marble palaces," and to watch the waves under their different aspects; now dancing joyously in the sunshine; then great sea-horses, foaming and dashing with terrible noise on the sands; now again, loveliest of all, lying at rest as if tired, in the solemn quiet of night, and giving back myriads of golden gleams for every star that twinkled in the clear Italian sky. And whilst Christopher thus watched the sea, he had very strange ideas for a young child, for he thought that the whole of the world had not been discovered, and that beyond the great Atlantic Ocean, which he had only heard of, there were lands that had never yet been trodden by Europeans. At the time he lived the Portuguese had discovered the Cape Verde Isles in the Atlantic, much of the western coast of Africa, and the Cape of Good Hope. They wanted some of the gold, amber, and ivory, the rich silks, and the fragrant woods and spices of India, and to trade in these things they had to find out a way to the East by sea, because the Venetians took care to keep the overland route to India clear for themselves. Venice, on the eastern side of Italy, and Genoa, on the western side, shared all the commerce of that country, but they were not on friendly terms; and for years and years the Genoese were trying to drive the Turks, Venetians, and Spaniards out of the Mediterranean Sea, that they might carry on their own commerce without being molested.

When Domenico Colombo found that his son Christopher had a very strong desire to be a sailor, he did not force him to pass his life in combing wool, but sent him to a famed school at Pavia, where he might learn such things as would be useful to him in the career he had chosen. So Columbus learned diligently about the earth, the sea, and the stars, and something of drawing and mathematics beside. When he was fourteen he returned to Genoa, and went to sea for the first time with one of his relations, who was likewise named Colombo. This man was a corsair, and had many a bold skirmish with the Turks and Venetians. During several years Christopher sailed with him from one place to another, and got used to a seafaring life. It happened in one of the skirmishes which took place between Lisbon and Cape St. Vincent, that fire broke out in a huge Venetian galley to which the vessel Christopher commanded for his kinsman had been chained during the fight; the flames quickly spread to the spot where he stood, and to save his life he was obliged to jump from the deck into the waves. Fortunately he had grasped an oar, and with this he was enabled to reach the shore of Portugal, at the distance of two leagues from the burning vessels. From thence he went to Lisbon, where he was kindly received by some Genoese, and he determined to remain in that city, because there were better means there of studying and of carrying out the plans he was making for a voyage in search of unknown lands. The Portuguese themselves were eager to make fresh discoveries: their mariners, sailing westward from the Azores, had seen floating on the waters corpses belonging to a race of men unknown in Europe, Africa, or Asia; besides these there were trunks and branches of strange trees, and huge sugar-canes which had been wafted through the Atlantic by the Gulf Stream. All these objects made them think that only a portion of the inhabited world had yet been revealed to them.

Two centuries had passed since Marco Polo, the bold Venetian explorer, had set out from Constantinople for the land of the Tartars. There he had found a friend in the great Kublai Khan, who ruled over Tartary and China, and was sent by him on a mission to China and India, being thus the first European who visited China Proper. On his return he told such extraordinary tales of the people he had seen, and their customs, that most men were afraid to believe in them, and thought they were pure inventions. Years after, when the countries he had described became known to the Europeans, it was found that he had spoken a great deal of truth, and his example caused fresh enterprises to be projected. Men must not despair because they do not at once see the fruit of their labour: if they only undertake it in a true and steadfast spirit, it is sure to turn sooner or later to the benefit of their fellow-creatures. Truly great men do not toil for themselves but for the good they may do to others; they sow the seed, and in God's time, not theirs, it will bear fruit.

In Lisbon Columbus married Doña Felippa, the daughter of a poor but noble Italian named Perestrello, the governor of the island of Porto Santo, one of the Madeiras, which had only lately been found. Perestrello was a very famous navigator, and lost his life in the service of Portugal. After his marriage Columbus went to live in the house of his wife's mother, and she gave him all the charts her husband had drawn, and the accounts he had written of his voyages, which proved very useful to him because they made him familiar with all the parts of the world the Portuguese had hitherto explored. So he lived on in Lisbon, supporting his wife and his mother by making and selling maps and globes, besides which he used to send a part of the money he earned to his aged father at Genoa, and helped his brothers also by enabling them to go to school. Sometimes he would leave home for a while, and take part in the expeditions that were directed towards the coast of Guinea, or he would visit Porto Santo, where he had a friend in Pietro Correo, who had once been governor of the island, and was married to his wife's sister. Yet although he was made very happy by the birth of his son Diego, it was sad to wait year after year without any chance of starting on his voyage; for, poor as he was, it was quite impossible for him to buy vessels and man them at his own expense.

Some of the ancient philosophers who flourished centuries before the birth of our Lord had convinced themselves that the earth was round. That such is the case is shown by the appearance of a vessel after it has left the shore. At a certain distance the whole of it is seen; farther off only its hulk or body; at a greater distance still, the topmast alone is visible. This proves that something hides the lower part of the ship from the spectator, and that something, is the roundness of the earth. Again—when an eclipse of the moon takes place the moon enters the shadow of the earth, and cannot get the light of the sun, which, reflected on her surface, gives her the bright silvery glow which makes her so lovely by night, and so we appear to lose the whole, or part of her face. Now the shadow that is seen being round, the earth must be round from which it is cast. And when men found, in the days when very long voyages were undertaken, that by sailing and journeying in one direction they came back to the point whence they had started, they wanted indeed no further proof that such was the correct figure of the earth. Thus it was natural for Columbus to expect to reach the eastern shore of India, or of Cathay (as China was then called) by sailing westward across the Atlantic, never dreaming that the earth was so large as it is, and that the pathway he went would make known to the people of the Old World the whole vast continent of America, and the Pacific, the greatest of all Oceans!

Having been refused assistance in his native city, he resolved at last to lay his plans before John the Second of Portugal. The king referred the matter to a Council, where it was soon decided that the voyage could not be carried out, but Columbus was not easily disheartened, as his patience during one-and-twenty years proved, and he begged the Portuguese monarch so earnestly to assist him that he had almost been supplied with the vessels he required, had there not been in Lisbon some persons who were very jealous of him, and wanted the glory of making the attempt themselves. These persons gained information of the proposed route, and then set out in secret to try it, not unknown, as it is said, to the king. But when they had been out at sea some time, and saw the waves spread out around them as far as sight could reach, they lost all courage, and put back to Lisbon as quickly as they could, saying on their return that the voyage could never be tried.

Columbus was indignant at being treated thus: he had passed fourteen years of his life in waiting, and had thought and studied so much for the enterprise on which he had set his heart that he had made no fortune for himself. His gentle wife Felippa was dead; and one day he bid farewell to his home in Lisbon and quitted Portugal with the idea of laying his cause before Ferdinand and Isabella of Spain. First of all, however, he went to Genoa, where he saw his father, and provided out of his own scanty means for the old man's comfort.

When he arrived in Spain he sought the favour and assistance of two powerful Spanish nobles, the duke of Medina Sidonia and the Duke of Medina Cœli. The latter was the kinder of the two; he was just going to give Columbus three or four caravels, which lay opposite the port of Cadiz when he suddenly thought that the enterprise was so vast, that none but a king should direct it. He spoke so kindly, however, of Columbus to Queen Isabella, that she desired him to repair to her court at Cordova.

When he arrived he found the city like a camp, and the king and queen entirely occupied in preparing for a grand campaign against the Moors. One Moorish city after another had indeed yielded to the Spanish arms, but the invaders who had held ground in Spain for nearly eight hundred years, were still in possession of much of the southern part of the country. At such a moment Isabella had no time to listen to the demands of a needy adventurer like Columbus, and his humble dress and his poverty made him an object of contempt in the eyes of the haughty Spanish grandees. At last, through the efforts of the Grand Cardinal of Spain, he was allowed to enter the presence of Ferdinand. The king ordered him to plead his cause before a great council of learned monks at Salamanca. During the time it was held, Columbus was a guest in the convent of St. Stephen, which was the foundation of the famous university of Salamanca. The monks of the convent were kind to him; they entered into his plans, and believed that the voyage he proposed would lead to great discoveries; and prove the source of infinite benefit to mankind; but those who came to confer with them were not of the same opinion, and they tried, by quoting the Holy

Scriptures, to convince Columbus that he was in error. Now Columbus was a very devout man, and one strong inducement for him to undertake the voyage was, the hope of spreading the gospel in distant parts of the world, and he must have been greatly pained when sentence was passed against him, and his views except by a few, were misunderstood and treated as idle dreams. Nevertheless he lingered on in Spain, in the hope that his appeal for aid might be heard one day by Isabella herself, who was of a more noble and generous character than her husband. So he followed the court from place to place as the seat of war changed, and in one campaign he bore an honourable part in the struggle with the Moors; while part of the time he remained in Spain he lived quietly at Cordova, earning his bread by making charts, and maps, as he had done before at Lisbon. When he heard that the city of Granada, the stronghold of the Moors, was to be invested by the Spanish army, he determined to make one more appeal, for he was sure that the king and queen would be too busy to listen to him, when the siege had once begun. All they would do was to promise to hear him when they should be released from the cares of war, and Columbus, grieving to think that he had wasted so many years of his life in useless waiting, made up his mind to leave Spain for ever, and apply for aid at the court of France.

From the time he left Cordova little is known of him until he appeared at the gate of the Convent of St. Maria de Rabida, which stood in the midst of a forest of pine trees, near the port of Palos, in Andalusia. His son Diego was with him; the boy was both tired and hungry, for they had come a long way without resting. Just as Columbus was asking for some bread and water for him at the gate, Friar Juan Perez, the guardian of the convent happened to pass by. The good friar welcomed the strangers kindly; he bade them enter, and in the course of conversation Columbus opened his heart to him and told him about his plans, and his firm trust that by the grace of God he should be able to carry them out. Friar Juan had already thought on the subject himself, and he was so delighted with the ideas of Columbus that he sent for two friends to confer with him: one was Fernandez Garcia, a physician of Palos, who had a great longing to go in search of unknown lands; the other was Martin Alonzo Pinzon, a merchant who had vessels of his own, and traded with many foreign ports. These were presently joined by some mariners of Palos, who had had much experience at sea.

Friar Juan persuaded Columbus to stay a little longer in Spain, and wrote a letter to Queen Isabella, hoping that his influence might induce her to sanction the enterprise, since he had once been her confessor, and had always been held by her in great esteem. The court had removed to Santa Fé, and an honest pilot, named Sebastian Rodriguez, undertook to convey the letter thither. At the end of a fortnight he brought back an answer from the queen which gave hope and joy to Columbus and his friends, and caused Friar Juan to saddle his mule in haste, and set out at midnight for the Spanish court. Isabella was indeed beginning to think the voyage worthy of consideration, and wished to talk on the subject with Juan himself. And very soon she summoned Columbus to Santa Fé, and sent him some money to enable him to buy a mule for his journey, and a dress suitable to appear in at court, so that he might no longer be despised for his needy attire.

Columbus arrived in time to see Boabdil, the last of the Moorish kings in Spain, deliver the keys of the Alhambra into the hands of the Spanish sovereigns: the hundred thousand Moors, who had shut themselves up within the massive walls of Granada, had been forced to yield; the Crescent was thrown down, and the Royal standard of Spain was planted on the red towers of the most beautiful of Moorish palaces. There were rejoicings and festivities without end among the Spaniards, but Columbus was sad and forlorn in the midst of all the gaiety; the courtiers were jealous of the favour Isabella had shown him on his arrival, and although the king and queen kept their promise and listened to him once more, they were persuaded, by a haughty and powerful priest named Talavera, now Bishop of Granada, to offer him terms which he could not accept. He began to feel utterly disheartened, and resolving again to leave Spain and ask help from France, he mounted his mule and quitted Santa Fé. He had reached the pass of Pinos, two leagues from Granada, when to his surprise a courier overtook him and recalled him to the Court. Some of his friends had at last persuaded Isabella to grant him real assistance, and she became all at once so eager for the voyage to be carried out, that she declared her kingdom of Castille should defray the cost of it, and offered to pledge her own jewels to furnish money besides.

The king and queen then signed a decree by which Columbus was to be supplied with vessels and men; to be named Admiral of the Fleet, and Viceroy of all the lands he should discover; and to have a right to a tenth part of all the gold, silver, pearls, precious stones, and spices he might find within the limits of the land he was to rule over for the Spanish sovereigns. Besides this the title of Don was to be prefixed to his name and to the name of his heirs.

All the doubts, the long weary days of waiting, were at an end. In deep thankfulness and joy Columbus went back to Palos, from which port it was arranged that the fleet should set sail. And one May morning a Royal decree was read in the porch of the largest church there which ordered the authorities of Palos to have two caravels [12] ready for the sea within ten days, Columbus himself having the right to fit out a third vessel.

But now his troubles broke out afresh, no one would furnish barks, not a mariner could be pressed into the service; it was believed that all who engaged in such a voyage must surely perish. After tumults and disputes which lasted many weeks, Martin Pinzon and his brother came forward with a vessel of their own, and two other caravels were with the greatest difficulty procured.

Thus the days which still elapsed before the fleet could sail, so full of joy and hope for the Admiral, were passed by the sailors and the friends they were to leave on shore in terror and deep gloom. At last, on Friday, August the 3rd, in the year 1492, the caravels sailed at daybreak from the bar of Saltes, near Palos, having on board one hundred and twenty persons, who before starting had all joined in fervent prayer that God would protect them from danger, and grant them success. A favourable wind bore them in the direction of the Canary Islands. The vessel Columbus sailed in was called the *Santa Maria*; the second, the *Pinta*, was commanded by Martin Alonzo Pinzon, and the third, the *Niña*, by his brother Vincent Yañez Pinzon. When they had been out at sea three days the *Pinta* made a sign of distress; either by accident or through malice to Columbus her rudder had been broken. Martin Pinzon repaired it as well as he could with cords, but the next day the wind broke them, and all the vessels put in towards the Canary Islands, and waited thereabouts three weeks whilst a new rudder was made for the damaged bark. This occasioned much loss of time, and news being brought that some Portuguese ships were sailing towards the Island of Ferro, Columbus set sail again in a great hurry, fearing that the jealousy of the King of Portugal might even now prevent him from finishing his voyage. For three days the caravels were held in a deep calm, and all the men on board felt very anxious until the winds arose, and carried them on their way. The last land they saw was the Island of Ferro, and when they lost sight of that, the spirits of most of the mariners began to droop, and a wreck which they came upon a hundred and fifty leagues from Ferro, did not tend to make them more hopeful.

On the 14th of September they saw a heron and a water wagtail, which very much surprised them, as they were the first birds they had seen. The next night there fell from the sky, only four or five leagues from the vessels, a wonderful stream of fire, although the sea was calm, and the winds were asleep, and the currents steady to the northward. This was probably one of the meteors which are often seen in warm climates. After that, from day to day, they perceived an abundance of grasses and herbs on the surface of the water—which appeared to have been plucked only a short time before from some island or rock—the green patches looked almost like floating islands themselves. Then they saw many tunny and gold fish, and a white

bird of the tropics that never passes a night on the sea. They thought, too, that the waves were less salt than those they had crossed at first. All these signs made the mariners very desirous of going in search of islands, but Columbus would not yield to their wishes, and pursued the steady course he had planned towards the west. On the 18th of September the captain of the swift-sailing caravel *Pinta* told the Admiral that he had seen a number of large birds flying towards the north, and that he thought there was land in that direction. This time, however, Columbus felt sure that the supposed land was nothing but a bank of clouds. The next morning a bird of the tropics alighted on the Admiral's ship, and the day after two more came with a black bird which had on its head a tuft of white feathers; besides which, at dawn, three little singing birds had perched themselves on one of the masts, and only flew away at dark. Their sweet song must have made some of the forlorn mariners think of their homes and the pine forest of Palos and the gardens of southern Spain, with their orange and pomegranate trees, whilst to others it may have said, "God, in His infinite love, has sent the little birds to cheer your hearts, and to tell you that land is near, and that you need not fear to tread the shore of strange men, since He is the father of all."

There came a time, indeed, when these things vanished, and as the wind always blew from the east, the men despaired of ever being able to return to their homes. They began to reproach Columbus bitterly for having led them, as they supposed, on a lost track, and distrusted the signs of land even when they were renewed by fresh patches of verdure appearing, and whole flights of singing birds coming to the caravels early in the morning, and flying away to their unseen nests at dusk. Some of the seamen in their frenzy were so wicked as to make a plot to throw the Admiral overboard, and they meant after that, to turn the vessel homeward, and to say, if they ever got back to Spain, that he had fallen from the ship's side whilst gazing at the stars. Columbus had enough to do to pacify the crews. To the gentle he spoke kind words; those who were eager for riches he flattered with hopes of gain, and the most violent of all he threatened with the severest punishment if they should attempt to prevent the voyage from being completed. At this time he was exposed to extreme danger, but he had a brave heart, and trusted in God, and did not feel afraid even when he knew that the plot had been made to take away his life. And although he was more anxious than any man on board, and passed many a sleepless night, looking vainly across the starlit sea for land, he never despaired of finding it at last.

So the days passed in alternate hope and fear. Once Martin Pinzon felt so sure that he saw land, that the crews of each vessel knelt down and chanted a solemn thanksgiving, "Glory to God in the highest," such were

the words that rose up in the calm evening air, but, alas! the land turned out to be only a cloud.

When the mutiny was at its greatest height the heavenly Father let the men who had murmured look on the blessed signs of land until their wicked thoughts passed away, and hope and trust came back to their hearts instead. For, on the 10th of October, there could be no doubt that they were near some shore. Beside fresh herbs and grasses, they saw a green fish, which is only found near rocks, a reed and a carved stick, a little plank, and a branch of thorn covered with red berries, which looked as if it had only just been plucked.

Columbus pointing to the Land.

After evening prayer on that day Columbus ordered a careful watch to be made, and remained himself on the high stern of the *Santa Maria* during the night. Now and then he observed a glimmer of light, which he supposed came from the shore, and at two o'clock in the morning the firing of a gun from the *Pinta* was the signal that land had really been seen. Not an eye closed that night; the sails were taken in, and the whole company on board the caravels waited in breathless suspense for the dawn. As the day broke, Columbus perceived a level island stretching out before them covered with trees; the natives were already coming out of the woods and rushing towards the shore, evidently astonished at the sight of the strange vessels. The boats were manned and armed, and Columbus, Martin Pinzon, and Vincente, his brother, each got into a boat, Columbus bearing the royal standard of Spain, and the others banners with green crosses upon them. The natives stood around as they landed, and looked on, half fearful, in silence. Columbus kissed the earth on which he first set foot, and planting the cross upon it, called it by the name of St. Salvador. [13] Then the Spaniards hailed him as Admiral, and swore obedience to him: those who had rebelled were now thoroughly ashamed of their wicked conduct, and entreated his pardon—a pardon he readily granted—for it was not in his noble nature to resent an injury done to himself.

The Spanish government had decreed a reward of 10,000 maravedis [14] to him who should first discover land; to this Columbus added a promise of a doublet of silk or velvet. But although Rodrigo de Triana was the mariner who first saw land from the *Pinta,* it was agreed by all that the Admiral should have the prize, because it was he who had perceived the light, probably of some torch the natives had carried, at intervals, during the night.

The island Columbus first landed upon was one of the Lucayos or Bahamas; in his delight he fancied he had really reached the eastern shores of India, and hence it was that the natives of the New World were called Indians. He stayed a day or two at the island, making friends with the dark-complexioned men, who soon lost all fear of the strangers, and regarded with great curiosity the cups, glass beads, and hawks' bells they gave them in exchange for the parrots, the balls of spun-cotton, and the cassava bread, made from a great root called "yuca," which they brought down to the shore. They were simple in their manners, and evidently thought the shining armour and weapons of the white man very strange. They did not know the use of iron, and taking the swords by the blades they cut themselves with them. Some of them wore little ornaments of gold in their noses, and when the Spaniards asked them by signs whence they got the gold, they answered by pointing to the south.

Columbus now resolved to go in search of the precious metal, and left the island, taking with him seven Indians as interpreters. When he returned to his ship the natives crowded around him in their canoes, each of which, small or large, was made in one piece out of the trunk of a tree. After finding some little islands, he came upon the lovely island of Cuba. Here the caravels glided down a great shining river, with waters deep and clear, and anchored not far from the sea. It seemed to the mariners a fairy region, in which they forgot all the care and the terror of their voyage. Trees, higher than any they had seen in Europe, were covered with the most tempting fruits and brilliant flowers, birds of gay-coloured plumage sang on their branches or flitted about. The sunshine falling on the scales of the fish made them look like precious stones, and at night, fireflies flashed through the air, and moon and stars shone with a strange lustre unknown in Europe. The cabins of the natives of Cuba were more elegant in their construction than those of the other islands, and were all well covered with branches of palm trees. That the people were accustomed to fish was shown by the nets, made of the fibres of palm leaves, which were found in some of the empty dwellings. Here was seen for the first time the "batata," or potatoe plant, which has since proved such a blessing to Europe, and some Spaniards, whom Columbus, believing that he had indeed reached Cathay, sent on a mission to the Grand Khan, tell how, when they came back from their fruitless journey, they met on the road numbers of people, men and women, who held in one hand a lighted brand, and in the other some leaves of a plant called "tabacas," rolled up in the form of a little cylinder, one end of which they lighted and the other they put into their mouths. It is needless to say that this was the origin of smoking amongst the Europeans, and hence the city of Havannah in Cuba has always been famous for the manufacture of cigars.

One night when the caravels were out at sea, not far from Cuba, on a voyage of fresh discovery, the *Pinta* suddenly disappeared. The merchant Martin Alonzo Pinzon was greedy of gain, and wanted to go to some island in search of gold by himself. One reason of his desertion is said also to have been his dislike of serving under another, after having been his own master for so many years. Columbus had now only the two caravels, but he was not deterred from making fresh attempts, and he soon found the large island of Haiti, or Saint Domingo, to which he gave the name of Hispaniola, because it was like the fairest parts of Spain. The land here was mountainous and rocky, but the rocks rose up out of forests. The harbour the caravels entered was surrounded by great trees, most of them being covered with fruit, which gleamed red, green, and golden in the bright sunshine of the tropics. The natives were very timid at first, as those of Cuba had been, and fled from the coast on the approach of the strange vessels; but an Indian woman who was captured and carried on board the *Santa Maria* was treated so kindly that, when she went back to the shore, her own people began to lose all fear, and brought the Spaniards many gifts of fish, fruit, and roots, and their famed cassava bread. Another day, when Columbus was cruising about the island, and a gale was blowing, he saved an Indian from perishing as his fragile canoe, and the man thus rescued told the time tale of the kindness of the Spaniards. Columbus became very friendly with a chief, or cacique, named

Guacanagari, which is a terribly long name, and since he always remained true to the Spaniards I will only call him in future the faithful chief, to distinguish him from others in the same island. The Admiral had set out by sea to visit him in his own village, when a great disaster happened. It was Christmas Eve; the ocean was calm and smooth, and about an hour before midnight the caravel *Santa Maria* was only a league from the cacique's dwelling. Columbus, having passed many sleepless nights, had gone to rest; soon after the steersman, giving the helm in charge to one of the ship's boys, followed his example, and it was not long before the whole of the crew were sound asleep also. The vessel, thus left to a careless boy, was carried by currents on to a sandbank with such force that great seams opened in her sides. Some of the mariners, roused to a sense of their danger, got down into their boat, and in the confusion rowed off to the caravel *Niña*, which took them all on board. Soon the Admiral and the remainder of the crew had to take refuge there also; the *Santa Maria* was firmly fixed in the sands, and was of no farther use as a ship. When the cacique heard of the misfortune he shed tears, and kindly sent a number of men in canoes to the Admiral's assistance, and he helped himself to keep guard round the wrecked vessel, that none of the valuable stores it contained might be stolen.

Little boys who are safe at home at the merry Christmas-time with all whom they love, may think of this first Christmas of the brave and patient Admiral, passed amidst all the horrors of shipwreck, and remember that if a simple and ignorant heathen could thus afford kindly help and sympathy to the distressed, how much more love and charity ought not those to show who call themselves the followers of Christ!

The cacique came on board the *Niña* to visit Columbus, and a little while after, the Admiral went to his village in return. When he was there he had a cannon and a harquebuss fired to show the might of the European arms. The Indians were so terrified at the sound that they fell flat to the ground, but their spirits revived when they were told that such weapons would deliver them from the Caribs, who were constantly threatening and tormenting their chief.

The cacique gave Columbus many extraordinary presents; one was a mask of wood, with eyes, ears, and mouth gilded: the Indians were very fond of carving such masks. They were delighted with the gifts they received from the Spaniards, and most of all with the hawks' bells, dancing merrily to the tinkling they made. They had so little idea of the real value of things that a string of the commonest glass beads had far greater worth in their eyes than a coronet of solid gold.

Columbus now began to think of returning to Europe, but first of all he constructed a fort with the remains of the stranded vessel, to which he gave the name of Navidad, [15] in memory of the Christmas morning when his own life and the lives of his men had been so mercifully spared. Some of the Spaniards were to be left to guard the fort, and they were very glad to remain in the island; they had food in plenty, the natives were kindly disposed towards them, and to live at ease in a beautiful climate was far preferable to being tossed about on the stormy sea. When the moment of parting came, however, all were sorrowful, and they took a kindly leave of one another, wondering whether they would ever meet again.

Some time after Columbus had set out on his journey home, he came in sight of the *Pinta*. The merchant made many excuses for his desertion, but Columbus passed them over with few words, and the vessels kept company until the *Pinta* again disappeared one dark night during a terrific storm, which surprised the caravels far out in the open sea. When it was at its greatest height Columbus retired to his cabin, and wrote two copies of a description of the lands he had seen, then he wrapped them in wax, and put them into two casks, one of which he threw into the sea, and the other he placed on the poop of his vessel, that it might float if she sank.

The storm abated, but Columbus was not yet destined to return to Europe in peace. He had touched at the Island of St. Mary, one of the Azores, and half the crew had landed to return thanks to God for their escape from the tempest. As they were praying in a chapel they were seized by order of John of Portugal, to whom the islands belonged. The King had watched the movements of Columbus, and could not get over his jealousy of the Spaniards for having succeeded in their attempt.

After some trouble the seamen were set free, but even then another storm drove Columbus to seek shelter in the river Tagus, near the Rock of Cintra. Whilst he was there, King John invited him to his court, which he was holding in a lovely spot, called the Vale of Paradise, a few leagues from Lisbon. Certain it is, that however unkind he had been hitherto, he received Columbus as a friend, and treated him with honour, and would not listen to some wicked men around him, who advised him to put him to death.

When Columbus did arrive at Palos on the 15th of March, 1493, the people flocked in crowds to welcome him, and he journeyed like a prince to Barcelona, where the Spanish court had taken up its residence for a time. But his greatest triumph was when he had entered the gates of the city, and went slowly along the crowded streets, surrounded by the noblest knights of Spain, to the palace where Ferdinand and Isabella were seated under a golden canopy in readiness to receive him. And surely the people of Barcelona had never looked upon so strange a procession before. Six Indians in their wild costume marched on in front; the animals belonging to the islands, live parrots, and other gaily plumed birds, till then unknown in Europe, the golden ornaments and the weapons of the natives, strange plants, valuable resins and gums, all had their part in the show. When Columbus arrived at the palace the King and Queen would not suffer him to stand or kneel in their presence, but they knelt down themselves in the sight of all the people, and thanked God fervently for the wondrous spectacle before them, and the new world that the courage and constancy of a good man had given to Leon and Castille. Whilst Columbus remained in Spain he was treated with the highest esteem and honour, and his sons, Diego and Fernando were appointed pages to Prince Juan, the heir to the Spanish throne.

Martin Alonzo Pinzon arrived at the port of Palos on the evening of the day Columbus had landed amid crowds of welcoming faces. He was so jealous of his rival's glory, and so deeply mortified besides when he remembered his own mean conduct towards one who had always been kind to him, that he went on shore privately, and instead of taking part in the public rejoicings, repaired to his home, where he fell ill, and died soon after, as it is said, of grief.

In the autumn of the same year Columbus set out on his second voyage with a fleet of seventeen ships, and fifteen hundred men, amongst whom were *hidalgos*, merchants and adventurers, and several priests, intended to convert the Indians to the Christian faith.

On his way to Hispaniola he found some islands belonging to the group of the Antilles. The first one he saw he called Domenica, because he discovered it on a Sunday. After that he came to a large and fertile island, to which he gave the name of Guadaloupe, and there the Spaniards saw for the first time the pine-apple. But although they found plenty of luscious fruits and sweet water, which refreshed them after their voyage, they were not at all happy there because they perceived from the remains of human bodies hanging about the dwellings that the natives of the island were cannibals, or Caribs, who feasted on the flesh of their fellow creatures. Columbus was in great alarm for fear some of his crew who had strayed into the forests should fall victims to this horrible practice; but happily, most of the men were absent on some warlike expedition, and had left their women to guard the island, and the missing mariners found their way back to the sea-shore. Another of the larger islands discovered at this time now bears the name of Porto Rico.

When the fleet arrived about a league from the settlement of Navidad, all objects around were hidden in the darkness of night. Columbus felt very anxious to know if the men whom he had left to guard the fort were alive and in safety, and he had two guns fired off to announce his arrival. The echo died away in silence, no answer came, and a terrible fear filled his heart. About midnight some Indians came in a boat to the principal caravel, and asked to see the Admiral. They had brought him a present of gilded masks from the faithful chief, and told how he lay sick in a little village near, having been wounded in an affray with another chief named Caonabo, who dwelt on the mountains of Cibao, and was called "The Lord of the House of Gold," because of the abundance of gold in that region. These Indians gave very confused accounts of the Spaniards who had been left in the fort. Some of them were dead, they said, having been killed in a skirmish; others were dispersed. Columbus did not know what to think. Even when the day broke, the place seemed strangely silent and deserted, and at last he sent some of his people in a boat to the shore to gain tidings. Alas! the fortress was a heap of ruins, the comrades of other days had all disappeared without leaving a trace behind. Columbus soon learned that several of the Spaniards had been faithless to the trust reposed in them, and after quarrelling amongst themselves had gone off to the mountains of Cibao, tempted by the prospect of finding gold. The few who remained in the fort had been surprised by Caonabo. He had rushed down upon them with his warriors, and had burnt all the dwellings of the white men, although the faithful chief had done his best to help to defend them: Columbus heard from him that the reports of the fate of the Spaniards were true.

When the cacique visited Columbus on board his ship he was greatly astonished at the sight of the animals which had been brought out to the west, such as cattle, pigs and calves, but most of all the Indians wondered at the power and size of the horse, which was to tread their shores for the first time. Besides these, Columbus had brought to the island many domestic fowls, also vegetables and fruits which he hoped would flourish in the new soil; among the latter were oranges, lemons, and citrons, supposed to have grown originally in India and Persia, and to have been introduced into Europe by the Arabs and Moors.

Immediately on his arrival Columbus founded the city of Isabella on the north of the island. For a little time the work went on bravely, and then troubles arose. The provisions conveyed in the vessels were nearly all gone; the climate was found to be sultry and damp, and unhealthy for those who had lived in the drier air of Spain. The young *hidalgos*, who had come out in the hope of gaining riches and fame, were angry and disappointed that they did not find gold at once in abundance. To appease their murmurs,

Columbus sent a very bold cavalier named Alonso de Ojeda to explore the famed mountains of Cibao, with a band of men, of whom most were of noble birth. When they came back from their dangerous expedition, they told the Admiral that they had seen gold in plenty glittering in particles amongst the sands of the mountain streams, and in the beds of the torrents. Several ships returned about this time to Spain, bearing samples of the gold thus discovered, besides various fruits and plants unknown in Europe.

The complaints of the settlers were again breaking out, when Columbus, leaving the growing city of Isabella in charge of his brother Diego, who had accompanied him on the voyage, set out himself for the mountains of Cibao with four hundred men, well armed, and a great multitude of Indians. When they arrived at the foot of the mountain land, it was found that so large a force could not ascend the wild and difficult path which was used by the Indians, and some brave young Spanish gentlemen who had been used to all kinds of manœuvres in the wars with the Moors, and were very eager to win fresh renown, undertook to make a road by which the whole company could pass. Thus in a few hours, by dint of hard labour, the first road in the New World was constructed, and it was called in honour of those who had made it, "El Puerto de los hidalgos," "The Gentleman's Pass."

When they came to the gorge of the mountain an immense plain spread out before them covered with lovely flowers, and with trees rising out of it, such as the graceful palm with its slender stem and feathery plume at the top, and the wide-spreading mahogany-tree with its dense foliage. The air was so balmy, and the whole scene was so beautiful, that Columbus gave it the name of "Vega Real," which means Royal Plain.

As they went higher up the mountains the way became rougher, and they lost the sweet flowers and fruits which had afforded them so much delight. Some of them saw what it must be confessed gave them still greater pleasure, and that was the gold which sparkled in the sands of the streams. At the top of a steep hill they built a fort, which they called Fort St. Thomas, that there might be a place of refuge for those who should work the mines. Caonabo did not at all like his "golden house" to be thus invaded, and took his revenge, as will be seen hereafter. The Indians as yet were very willing to exchange gold for the glass beads and toys the Spaniards gave them, and would search for it on purpose to bring it to them. One old man parted with two pieces of gold which weighed an ounce, and thought he was magnificently paid for it with a hawk's bell.

When Columbus returned to Isabella, he found that the building of the city had been neglected: the workmen were either ill or weary of the task, and he gave orders that all who had come out to the island should assist in the labour. The proud Spanish *hidalgos* worked with very unwilling hearts, and never forgave Columbus for submitting them to what they considered a great degradation. Some of them were so disappointed with the New World and the difficulty of making themselves rich without any trouble that they fell ill and died, bitterly reproaching Columbus until their last hour as being the cause of all their misfortunes. These troubles made the Admiral very unhappy; still, amidst them all he had some joys, and one very great one, when after he had gone to coast along a part of Cuba unknown to him, he came upon the large island of Jamaica, with its high blue mountains and its groves of majestic trees. Jamaica thus ranks third of the great islands made known to the Europeans. Here the natives made each of their boats out of the single trunk of a tree, and when they used for this purpose the enormous stem of a mahogany tree they had a very large boat indeed.

Columbus did not stay long at Jamaica, but cruised about another part of Cuba, and found some smaller islands near its coast, which were so lovely that he called them "The Queen's Gardens." On his way back to Hispaniola he became very ill, and was senseless when his vessel reached the port of Isabella. Great was his joy, when he opened his eyes once more to find his brother Bartholomew by his bedside; he had been sent to the island by the Spanish sovereigns, and as he was very brave and clever he was well fitted to take the command of affairs whilst his brother was ill.

The troubles in the island rapidly increased. The chiefs, with the exception of the faithful one, were ready to make war on the Spaniards and drive them away. Caonabo was the fiercest of all; he lay siege to the Fort of St. Thomas, but Alonso de Ojeda was inside with a few brave men, and harassed his army so much by his firearms that the Indians at last withdrew in despair. Ojeda afterwards captured Caonabo in a very daring manner, and brought him bound to himself on his horse to the city of Isabella, where he was imprisoned in the Admiral's house. After this the Indians were ordered to pay tribute in gold dust, which at first only made them resist the more; it seemed so hard to them to have to work from morning to night in search of gold, after the free and happy life, happy for them because it was idle, they had lived in their island before the strangers came. It was not until a battle had been fought on the lovely plain of the Vega, and some of them had been killed by the firearms of the Spaniards, which were far more destructive than their own weapons, that they consented with heavy hearts to bring their tribute.

For everything that went wrong, Columbus alone was unjustly blamed, and at last some unkind persons went to Spain and told the King and Queen that he had brought all the misery on the colony by his bad government.

And a day came when he set out for Spain himself to plead his cause with Ferdinand and Isabella; because, whatever his enemies had said, his conduct had always been loyal and upright, and the cause of all the unhappiness lay in the violent temper and the avarice of many of the men who had embarked with him for the sake of making themselves rich, instead of serving the king and queen, and promoting the glory of Spain.

The vessel he sailed in was crowded with criminals, discontented persons and Indian captives; amongst the latter was the proud chief Caonabo, but he died during the voyage.

When Columbus arrived this time in Spain, there were neither triumphs nor rejoicings, and he wore as he landed the dress of a Franciscan friar, a long robe, with a cord for a girdle, in sign of humility. He was soon cheered, however, by a kind invitation to court. Ferdinand and Isabella did not yet forget how much they owed to him, and they gave no heed to the complaints that had been made against him, while the massive gold ornaments he had brought with him, and the rich products of the islands induced them to hope that his discoveries would bring them great wealth in the time to come.

He therefore lived in Spain in some degree of comfort until the May of the year 1498, when after many tiresome delays he started on a third voyage with only six ships and took a different route to that he had gone before. From the Cape Verde Isles he went south-west towards the region spreading out eight or ten degrees north and south of the Equator, where the sea is smooth as glass, and the sun shines straight down, and there is not a breath of air to fill a sail. The heat on this occasion was intense, and the mariners very nearly died of thirst when their supply of water was exhausted and they could get no more. Columbus therefore sailed westward, instead of going farther south as he had at first proposed, and one day, just three months after he had left Spain, three mountains seemed to rise up out of the ocean afar, and as he came nearer he found to his joy that all the mountains rose from one island, to which in his thankfulness he gave the name of Trinidad. [16]

On this voyage he also discovered the mouths of the river Orinoco, which it will be seen, by the map of South America, are not very far from the island of Trinidad. Still, Columbus did not think when he landed, that he was treading the shores of a vast new continent, but imagined that it was a part of Asia. After this he found the land the Indians called Paria. The natives here welcomed him kindly, and brought him bread and maize: they were tall and graceful, and their manners were gentle; they wore garments of cotton wrought so beautifully with colours that they looked like rich silks, and they carried targets besides bows and arrows. They had several kinds of liquors which they offered to the Spaniards to drink. One was "white as milk," made from maize; others were nearly black, and tasted as if they were made from unripe fruit.

The country was covered with flowers and fruit-trees; vines were twined from tree to tree and bright plumaged birds, chiefly parrots, flitted about. Some of the natives wore collars of gold around their necks, and some had bracelets of pearls, the sight of which gave great satisfaction to the Spaniards, for they thought they had discovered a new source of riches. Columbus would have liked to have spent much time in exploring the coasts of Paria, but his stores were nearly all consumed, and he was ill and almost blind from having strained his eye-sight during the dark nights of his voyages, and was therefore obliged to think of returning to Hispaniola or San Domingo, as it was called besides. Along the north coast of Paria he saw many islands, some of which afterwards became famous for their pearl fisheries, and in one little barren isle he got many beautiful pearls in exchange for hawks' bells, and pieces of broken china, which the Indians thought very precious.

At last, wearied out in mind and body he arrived at Hispaniola, hoping to rest for a while in peace, but he found the colony in a state of rebellion; a wicked man named Roldan, who had been raised to high estate by Columbus, persuaded the people to rise up against the Admiral of the Indies and his brothers: the mines were no longer worked, the building of the city was left unfinished, and there was scarcely any food. And now we come to the saddest part in the whole story of Columbus. Some wretched convicts who had been sent out of Spain to the island, and who were in league with Roldan, contrived to make their escape and return to Europe, where the false reports they spread reached the ears of Ferdinand and Isabella, and induced them to believe at last that he was not really worthy of the trust they had reposed in him. Francesco Bovadilla, a man who cared very little what he did, was therefore sent to Hispaniola with orders to govern the island in his stead, whilst Columbus himself was to be sent back to Spain.

It had happened that at the very moment the Admiral was going to embark on his third voyage he was deeply affronted by a follower of one of his worst enemies in Spain; and although he had endured many wrongs and injuries in a patient and forgiving spirit, he gave way this time to a violent fit of passion, and struck the time-serving creature repeatedly in his wrath. The news of this was of course conveyed to the King and Queen, and this one act of passion on the part of Columbus made them more inclined to believe in the reports of his ill conduct than all the complaints that had been spoken against him: they thought that if he were capable of such an action, there were more cruel and angry deeds to come; just as one little storm cloud hastening across the clear blue sky makes us dread that others, heavier and darker, are near.

As soon as Bovadilla arrived he settled himself in the Admiral's house, Columbus being absent at one of the forts, and laid hands on all the money, plate, jewels, and valuable things he could find. Columbus disdained to question the acts of an unruly man like Bovadilla, and journeying in haste and alone to St. Domingo, he calmly resigned his command. He was then put in fetters, although for a long time no one could be found who would fasten them. At last this shameful office was performed by one of his cooks, a Spaniard. His brother Diego was already in chains on board a caravel: Bartholomew would have resisted, but was advised by the Admiral to submit calmly, and the three brothers, who were so loving and could have comforted one another in their misfortunes, were all kept apart.

One day Columbus saw an officer named Villejo coming towards him in his prison followed by his guards.

"Where are you going to take me, oh, Villejo?" he asked.

"To the vessel, your Excellency, to embark," he replied.

"To embark!" exclaimed Columbus, radiant with joy. "Do you speak truth?"

"By the life of your Excellency I speak truth;" said he; and they went indeed on board the caravel which was to convey them to Spain.

During the voyage Villejo and the captain of the vessel were very kind to him, and were grieved to see him in chains; they would have removed them, but Columbus would not let them do so, saying that they had been placed upon him by order of the King, and his younger son Fernando tells us that his father, stung at last by a sense of his wrongs, kept them ever after hung up in his room as a sign of the manner in which he had been rewarded for his services. Yet let us hope that when he looked at them he forgave his enemies, since there are no injuries too deep to be forgiven, if we ourselves would receive pardon of our heavenly Father for our many misdeeds.

When Columbus landed at Cadiz thus shackled, a murmur of shame and indignation was breathed throughout Spain. Ferdinand and Isabella ordered his fetters to be removed at once, and sent him a large sum of money to pay the expenses of a visit to court. And when he appeared in their presence, bowed down by illness and age, and worn out with the dangers and misfortunes he had gone through, and he saw tears in the eyes of Isabella, who had once been his kindest friend, he knelt down and burst into a flood of tears himself. The Queen consoled him with gentle words, and tried to atone by her kindness for the many affronts he had suffered. Ferdinand always maintained that he had never given orders for Columbus to be fettered, and that Bovadilla had acted rashly on his own authority. Be that as it may, the King was a stern and narrow-minded man; he did not like to see a foreigner filling the important office of Viceroy of the Indies, and he took care never to reinstate Columbus in his former dignity, whilst he sent out a man named Ovando to govern Hispaniola instead of Bovadilla.

Columbus now formed the project of finding a strait somewhere about the Isthmus of Darien, which should prove a shorter route to India than the voyage by the Cape of Good Hope. Although he was getting feeble and aged he had the same steadfast spirit which had enabled him to wait patiently all the best years of his life, and had helped him bravely through all his troubles, and he wanted yet to be of farther service to his fellow-men before he died. The Portuguese under Vasco de Gama had already anchored opposite Calcutta, and the trade with India was thus all their own, while the discovery of the West Indian islands seemed to be less important. If anything more were to be done by Columbus it must be begun at once, and the King and Queen granted him four caravels with which to set out on his fourth and last voyage. The crews of all amounted to four hundred and fifty men. His brother Bartholomew was with him and his younger son Fernando; the elder one, Diego, being left to manage his affairs in Spain.

The little fleet was to have gone straight to Jamaica, but the principal vessel sailed so badly that it hindered the others, and Columbus steered instead for Hispaniola, hoping to exchange it for one of the fleet that had carried out Ovando. He also asked to be allowed shelter in the harbour of San Domingo, as he believed from certain signs in the atmosphere which he knew only too well, that a very great storm was near; but Ovando would neither let him have a vessel nor take shelter. Just at that time, the fleet which had brought out Ovando was ready to sail, and was to convey to Spain, the rebel and conspirator Roldan, Bovadilla, who had treated Columbus so ill, and many persons who had led idle and wicked lives in the island. They had with them a great quantity of gold, some of which had been gained by the labour and miseries of the Indians. Amongst the gold that Roldan was going to take to the King and Queen was one enormous solid lump, which was said to have been found by an Indian woman in a brook.

Although Columbus was denied shelter himself he sent a message to the port, warning the men who were about to sail of the approaching storm, and entreating them to remain in the harbour until it was over. Well had it been for them if they had listened to his advice, but they only laughed at it and boldly put out to sea. Before two days had passed a terrible hurricane arose, the tempest burst over the ships, and all those men who had been the greatest enemies of Columbus were swallowed up with their gold by the foaming waves. The few vessels which were not entirely destroyed returned to Hispaniola in a shattered condition; only one was able to reach Spain, and that strangely enough had on board a large sum of money which belonged by right to Columbus, and had been despatched to Spain by his agent.

Columbus kept close to the shore that night, but the tempest was terrible for him too; the caravels were dispersed and every one on board expected death, or thought that the others were lost. At last all the vessels, more or less damaged, arrived safely at Port Hermoso on the west of the island, and Columbus stayed there some days to repair them. During an interval of calm he reached the Gardens of Cuba, but soon after this his troubles began afresh. For forty days he coasted along Honduras, while the most fearful storms prevailed, and the whole time he could enter no port. The sea was tremendously high, heavy rains fell continually, and the thunder and lightning were so terrific that the mariners thought that the end of the world was coming; added to this the sails and rigging of the caravels were torn, and the provisions were spoiled by the damp. Columbus grieved that his son Fernando should be exposed to all these misfortunes. He says of him in a letter, "God gave him so great courage that he sustained the others, and if he put his hand to work, he did it as if he had been at sea for eighty years. It was he who consoled me; I had fallen ill and many a time was near the gate of the tomb. From a little cabin which I had caused to be constructed on the stern I directed the voyage. My brother was on the most wretched and dangerous of the vessels; great was my sorrow because I had brought him against his will." Then he goes on to tell all his troubles; and laments that although he had served Castille for so many years, he had not really a roof in the land he could call his own. He thought tenderly, too, of his son Diego, in Spain, and pictured the sorrow he would feel if he heard that all the vessels had perished. In the forty days the fleet only made seventy leagues; but at least they reached a cape where the coast made an angle and turned southwards, and the admiral in his joy and gratitude gave it the name of "Gracias a Dios." [17]

Now he sailed along the Mosquito shore, the rivers of which abounded with tortoises and alligators, and in one of these rivers they lost some of their men who had gone in a boat to seek for provisions. This cast a great gloom over the rest, which had not passed away when they came to a beautiful island full of groves of cocoa nuts, bananas, and palms, and rested awhile between it and the main land. The Indians on shore were very proud, for when the admiral refused the gifts they brought to the ship, they tied all the toys and bells the Spaniards had given them together, and laid them on the sands. When Columbus quitted the spot, he took seven of these Indians with him as interpreters, and coasted along Costa Rica for several leagues, until he entered a great bay full of lovely islands. The natives here wore large plates of gold hanging from chains of cotton cord around their necks, and strange crowns made of the claws of beasts, and the quills of birds. They told the strangers that about seventy leagues off they would find Veragua, a country which abounded in gold. And it seemed, indeed, as if they spoke the truth, for the nearer they came to that country the more gold they saw. The natives wore crowns of it on their heads, and rings of it round their wrists and ancles; their garments were embroidered with it; their tables and seats were ornamented with it. But Columbus had not come out this time in search of gold, but to find the strait which should enable Spain to trade with India at ease, and he left the land of promised riches and went on the way he thought would lead to his discovery. Alas! it was soon found that the caravels were too leaky to sail with safety; they had been pierced through by a worm which infests the tropical seas, and can bore through the hardest wood; [18] and Columbus was obliged to give up sailing, for the present, in search of the strait, and returned to seek for the gold mines of Veragua. [19] It was now December, and again the caravels were overtaken by one of the terrible storms of the tropics. The poor mariners gave themselves up for lost; day and night they confessed their sins one to another, and made vows of what they would do if their lives were spared. The lightnings were so incessant that the sky glowed like "one vast furnace;" and they saw, too, for the first time a water-spout, which, advancing towards the caravels, threatened them with destruction; but the Lord heard the prayers the terrified seamen sent up at the strange sight, and the column of water passed by without doing them any injury.

In the midst of the storm there was an interval of calm, during which they saw many sharks; these fishes are supposed to scent dead bodies at a distance, and often draw near ships when danger is at hand. The sailors caught some of them, and took out of one a live tortoise, which lived some time on board one of the vessels; from another they took the head of a shark, which shows that these monsters sometimes eat one another. In the history which Fernando wrote of his father, he says that the sufferings of all on board were very great for want of food; the provisions being spoiled by the damp, and they had to eat their biscuit in the dark, because it was so full of worms that it was too dreadful to behold by clear daylight.

At last they entered a port which the Indians called Hueva, and went from thence along a canal for three days. When they landed they found the natives living in the trees like birds, their cabins being fastened to poles which were suspended from one tree to another. Perhaps they did this on account of the wild beasts, the forest being full of lions, bears, racoons, tiger-cats, and sajinos, a species of wild boar which attack men. After a while the caravels anchored in the mouth of a river which was really in the country of the gold mines. The admiral sent his brother on shore to explore the land; and as he soon satisfied himself that there was gold to be found there in plenty, Columbus at once began to form a settlement on the river, which he called Belen, or Bethlehem, after the star the wise men had seen in the east, because the caravels had arrived there on the Feast of the Epiphany. It was agreed that Bartholomew should remain here while the admiral returned to Spain to procure fresh vessels and supplies. So they built houses of wood, thatched with the leaves of palm trees, on a little hill not far from the mouth of the river, and eked out their scanty store of provisions with the pine-apples, bananas, and cocoanuts, which grew around them in plenty; and drank the wine the Indians made from the pine-apple, and a sort of beer prepared from maize, or Indian corn. When the rains ceased, however, Columbus found that the river was so shallow, his crazy and worm-eaten ships could not get out and cross the bar, so that he was obliged to wait patiently until the rains should swell the river again and set him free.

Now it happened that Quibain, the chief of the district, was very angry when he saw the Spaniards had taken up their abode in his country, and ordered all his fighting men to be ready to drive them away. A brave man named Diego Mendez offered to reconnoitre the Indian camp, and soon returned to tell Columbus that he had seen a thousand Indians who seemed to be arrayed for battle. After this, with only one companion, he contrived to get to the chief's village, pretending that he was a surgeon, and could cure a wound Quibain had received in some skirmish. As he approached the house a horrible sight awaited him; for on a level plain in front of it the heads of three hundred men were fixed on poles. This was enough to give a terrible idea of the fury of Quibain, if it were once roused. Mendez was not allowed, however, to enter the cacique's dwelling; and went back to the settlement to tell Columbus what he had seen, and the news he had heard that the Indians were coming to burn their houses and ships.

Now, as we have said before, Bartholomew Columbus was a very brave man, and he set out from Belen with Diego Mendez, and about seventy armed men in boats, and soon landed at the foot of the hill on which the chief dwelt. Then he ascended the hill with only Diego and four men besides, ordering the others to rush forward at the firing of a gun. Bartholomew went alone to the spot where Quibain was sitting in the open air, and pretending to look at his arm, held it tight until his comrade fired the gun which should summon the rest. He had much ado to hold the chief in his grasp, but he kept firm until he was bound hand and foot. The house was soon surrounded, and all the family of Quibain were taken prisoners without the shedding of a drop of blood; and Bartholomew returned to the settlement laden with spoils, amongst which were many massive gold ornaments, and two coronets of gold.

Quibain was committed to the care of the pilot of the fleet, and was tied by a strong cord to a bench in the pilot's boat. In the darkness of night the chief complained of the tightness of the cord, and the pilot, touched with pity, loosened it, holding the end of it in his hand. When he was looking another way for a moment, the wily Indian plunged into the water and disappeared; the pilot of course was obliged to let go his hold or he would have been pulled in after him.

Columbus now thought that since the greatest enemy of the Spaniards had thus perished, and the river was again filled by the heavy rains, he might safely return to Spain, and he sailed out of the harbour. But Quibain had not been drowned; he swam cleverly to the shore, and when he found his house deserted, he assembled all his warriors, intending to take his revenge. Some of the Spaniards who were to remain were straying carelessly about, when these wild men rushed out of their hiding places in the deep woods, and killed and wounded several of them. Bartholomew and Mendez soon drove them back with their fire arms; but Diego Tristan, the captain of one of the vessels, who had gone on shore with eleven men to get wood and water, was cruelly killed by the Indians, and only one Spaniard of the whole party survived to tell the tale. So the remainder shut themselves up in a fortress they made of a boat and some chests and casks, and defended themselves as well as they could by their fire arms.

Columbus, meanwhile, was pursuing his voyage, and meant to touch at Hispaniola on his way to Spain. Some of the Indian captives who were on board his ship, escaped; the others killed themselves in their despair. Diego Tristan not having returned to the admiral's vessel with his boat, a brave pilot swam to the shore and gained tidings of all that had happened. Columbus now resolved to break up his settlement, and take all his people back to Spain, but even this he could not do for a very long time. First of all a storm arose, as terrific as the previous ones had been: he was in the deepest anxiety, when one night he had fallen asleep, he heard, in a dream, a voice that consoled him for all that he had suffered, and reminded him of the never-failing mercy of God, so that when he awoke he had fresh hope and courage in his heart.

And before long there was a calm, which enabled him to reach the fortress where his brother and his brave comrades were in such great distress. The caravel that was with them was too much damaged to be of farther use, and they were obliged to leave it behind. Thankful indeed were the Spaniards to leave the country of Veragua, where they had gone through so many troubles and left many of their countrymen lying dead. They embarked in the three vessels that were left, but one of these was soon found to be in a very dangerous condition, and the whole company crowded on two wretched caravels. They could not reach Hispaniola on account of the storms, and were glad to put into the harbour of St. Gloria, at Jamaica, where they gave up the struggle. The two vessels were now run aground and tied together, and cabins were constructed at the prow and stern, which were the only parts of the caravels above water. They were thatched with straw, to keep out the rain, and here for one long year Columbus remained with his crew, forsaken and in much misery. The Indians indeed brought them cassava bread, and fish and flesh, for which they gave them the usual toys and beads; but how were they to make known their distress to Ovando, that he might send vessels to their relief? At last the brave and faithful Mendez, the only one who would undertake such a perilous journey, ventured in a canoe with six Indians and one Spaniard to reach the island of Hispaniola. The first time he tried he was surrounded by the savages and carried off by them, but he contrived to make his escape and returned alone to the harbour: it is not known what became of his companions. The second time he tried he succeeded in reaching the island. During his absence a number of the crew rebelled; Columbus, rising from his sick bed, endeavoured vainly to pacify them, but they forsook him and went on shore, where they behaved very ill to the Indians.

Eight months passed before Columbus received any tidings of Mendez, and he began to fear that he had been killed by the savages or had perished in his frail canoe. At last a messenger came from Hispaniola, and said that Ovando would send a vessel for the forlorn band as soon as he had one large enough to hold them all. When Columbus knew that they would be rescued, in the greatness of his soul he offered a free pardon to the men who had rebelled, and offered to take them safely to Spain if they would return to the path of duty; all that he required was that their ringleader should be kept a prisoner. But this bad man would not let them accept the pardon, and persuaded some of the Indians to join them and take up their weapons against Columbus. Bartholomew, of the martial spirit, had to go on shore and quell the disturbance by force; after this their spirit was broken, and they confessed their misdeeds and asked Columbus to forgive them. Ovando sent two vessels, and Columbus then took them all on board and gave them money to buy food and clothing, of which they were in sore need: he succoured alike those who had been faithful throughout and those who had rebelled, remembering how the merciful Lord maketh the sun to shine on all.

On his way to Spain he touched at St. Domingo, and embarked afresh. Scarcely had he left the shore when the mast of his ship was carried away by a squall. Storms went with him all the way home, and he was wearied out with pain and anxiety when he anchored in the harbour of St. Lucar, never more to sail on the sea he loved so well.

He only lived eighteen months after his arrival. The remainder of his life may be told in a few sad words. Queen Isabella, his friend and patron, died only a few days after his return to Spain. The King refused to listen to his claim for the just reward of his services and those of his brave companions, and it reflects no honor on the Spanish monarch that he allowed him to pass the last days of his useful life in poverty and neglect.

On Ascension day, the 6th of May of the year 1506, Columbus died at Valladolid. Friends were around him as he sank to rest, saying, with his last breath, "Lord, into thy hands I commend my spirit." And it may be that the hardships he had endured, and the insults and reproaches of his fellow-men, made him long more earnestly for that better land, fairer than the loveliest island that had risen up from the ocean before his astonished gaze, the land of the redeemed, where "the Lamb which is in the midst of the throne shall feed them, and shall lead them into living waters; and God shall wipe away all tears from their eyes."

As if to make amends for the neglect he had experienced whilst on earth his remains were interred with great pomp in the convent of St. Francis at Seville. They were removed three times after that, and now rest in the cathedral of the Havannah at Cuba. He made by his will his son Diego his heir, and ordered that one of his family should always reside at Genoa, which shows that he preserved an affectionate remembrance of his native city until the last days of his life.

His son Fernando tells us that he had a long face, a bright complexion, an aquiline nose, and lively eyes of clear grey, which seemed to enforce obedience. His hair was fair in his youth, but began to turn white when he was only thirty years of age, which made him look much older than he really was. He was very frugal, and dressed with great simplicity. Although naturally hasty in temper he treated all persons around him with extreme gentleness and kindness, and was always ready to succour those who were in trouble or need. He was sincerely religious, and never omitted to praise and to pray to God during his voyages either morning or night. In calm weather and in stormy the voices of the mariners chanting their matins and vespers rose from the lonely sea. Sunday to him was always a day of rest, and he would never set sail on that day if he could avoid doing so.

This chapter ought not to end without the relation of the well-known story of Columbus and the egg. One day, after his triumphal return from his first voyage, he was dining at the table of the Grand Cardinal of Spain, and one of the grandees present asked him if he did not think others could have found out the way to the new shore as well as himself. Upon this Columbus took an egg, and asked each person present to make it stand on the table. Not one being able to do so, Columbus took the egg, and, breaking one end of it, made it stand upright. Then he said that if one showed the way it was easy enough for others to follow in his steps, just as the company assembled could each make the egg stand on the table now that he had shown them how to do it.

FOOTNOTES:

[12] A caravel was a small light bark, more fitted to sail on a river than to cross the stormy seas.

[13] Salvador, Spanish for Saviour.

[14] A copper coin of Spain, thirty-four of which are worth one real.

[15] *Navidad*, Spanish for Nativity.

[16] Trinidad, Spanish for Trinity.

[17] Gracias a Dios, Spanish for "Thanks be to God."

[18] See Washington Irving.

[19] Now called Panama.

THE CHEVALIER DU BAYARD

Pierre de Terrail Bayard was born in the year 1475, at the castle of Bayard, in Dauphiné. His ancestors had long been feudal lords of the part of the province whence they took their name, and were always renowned for their valour and loyalty. The great-great-grandfather of Pierre died in the Battle of Poictiers at the feet of his king, John of France: his great-grandfather fell at Cressy; his grandfather at Monthéri; and his father received so many wounds in an action with the Germans that he could never after leave his Castle of Bayard. And when he was getting feeble, and felt that his days were numbered, he called his four sons around him, and asked each one of them what state of life he would choose for himself.

The eldest replied that he would like always to live at the old Castle of Bayard, amongst his own people; so his father said to him, "Very well, George, since you are so fond of home, you shall stay here and fight the bears." Pierre, the second son, then thirteen years old, said that he desired to follow the profession of arms, as his father had done; and that he trusted through the grace of God to acquit himself with honour therein. The third son said he would like to have an abbey, like his uncle, the Monseigneur of Esnay, and the youngest wished to be a bishop, like his uncle of Grenoble.

The Sire du Bayard rejoiced very much at the choice little Pierre had made, but as he could not decide at once where he should be trained for the service of his country, he sent in haste for his brother-in-law, the Bishop of Grenoble, that he might tell him the glad news and ask his advice in the matter.

The bishop came, and made good cheer at the Castle, several gentlemen of Dauphiné having been invited thither to render him honour. He was as much delighted as the Sire du Bayard at the thought that Pierre would maintain the glory of his ancestors, and the day after his arrival advised that he should enter the service of Charles, Duke of Savoy. The Duke was then at Chambéry, a place not far from the Castle, and the Bishop of Grenoble proposed taking his nephew to him the next morning.

Thus it was settled that little Pierre should leave his home for ever, and part with his brothers, his merry playmates in the woods and fields around

Bayard, and his gentle mother, who loved him perhaps above all her other sons; but his father felt that he was getting weaker every hour, and since he was not rich, he was very anxious to provide for the welfare of his children as far as he could before he died.

First of all, however, it was agreed that Pierre must be equipped as a page, and the Bishop sent for his own tailor, bidding him bring with him satin and velvet, and all that was necessary for a page's dress in those days. The tailor had to work hard all night, and the next morning, Pierre in his new habit went down into the courtyard and mounted a war-horse, which stood there ready saddled, while his father and all his guests looked on from the lower windows of the Castle. The horse feeling so light a burden upon him grew restive, and it seemed each moment as if Pierre must have been thrown, but to the delight and astonishment of all who beheld him, the boy, who had left school only a fortnight before, managed his horse, as an old French writer tells us, with as much skill as if he had been thirty years of age.

The Sire du Bayard now bid him not to dismount, and gave him his blessing, after which all the rest of the people took leave of him. Pierre's eyes filled with tears when his father looked so proudly and lovingly at him. "Monseigneur, my father," he said, "I pray to our Lord to give you a long and happy life, and to me grace, so that before you quit this world, you may hear good news of me."

In the meantime his mother was weeping alone in a turret chamber of the Castle; for although she was glad that he had chosen to follow a soldier's life for the honour of his name, she grieved bitterly at the thought of parting with him, and feared that she should never see him again. She came down into the courtyard by a back staircase, and there took leave of him with many tears, and gave him words of advice which he remembered so well all his life long that he gained both from his friends and from his foes the title of "The good knight, without fear and without reproach."

These were some of the words she said: That he was to love and serve God, without giving Him offence, as far as in him lay; and that he could do no good work in this world without His help and blessing. That he was to be gentle and courteous to all, casting away pride; humble, ready to serve his fellow creatures, and sober in eating and drinking. That he was never to tell a lie, or flatter, or be a tale-bearer, or be idle; that he was to be loyal in deed and speech, to keep his word; to succour the widows and orphans, for which the Lord would repay him, and that he was to share with the needy such gifts as God might bestow upon him, since giving in honour of Him made no man poor.

When the noble lady had spoken thus, she gave her son a little purse, which contained a few pieces of gold, and then having implored a trusty servant of the Bishop's to be careful of him, because he was so very young to leave home, she bade him a last farewell.

The day after Pierre's arrival at Chambéry was Sunday. After mass, a great banquet was served in honour of the Bishop of Grenoble, who was a very holy man, and much beloved by the Duke of Savoy. During the repast Pierre stood beside his uncle and poured out his wine for him, and when it was ended he did not linger over the remains of the feast with the pages and youths belonging to Duke Charles's household, but hastened back to his lodgings and saddled his horse, and having mounted it, went down to the courtyard of the palace.

The Duke had remarked his graceful bearing during dinner, and now seated in a gallery was watching him in the court below. Then the Bishop told him how the Sire du Bayard, being too much enfeebled by his wounds to lift his sword again, had sent his little son Pierre to him as a gift, and hoped that he would allow him to enter his service. The Duke of Savoy said that the present was both good and fair, and agreed to take young Bayard into his service without delay. So the Bishop returned home, and Pierre was left alone amongst strangers. He must have sorrowed at first for the old life at Castle Bayard, and the watchful love of his mother, but whatever he felt, he began to fulfil his duties with an earnest heart, and was kind and gentle to all around him, and never forgot to pray morning and night that the Almighty would give him grace to remain loyal and brave. Pierre lived with the Duke at Chambéry for six months, and during that time he made himself beloved by every inmate of the house: he was a great favourite with the Duchess of Savoy, and had one little playmate, amongst the young maidens who were in attendance upon her, to whom he was much attached.

When the six months had expired the whole party set off on their mules, according to the custom of travelling at that time, to visit King Charles the Eighth in the city of Lyons. The king, struck with the reports he had heard of Bayard's conduct, and the knightly grace he displayed in his presence, made him his own page, and had him lodged in the house of the Seigneur de Ligny, a prince of the house of Luxembourg, to be trained with about thirty other noble youths in the use of arms.

There was a squire belonging to the household of the Duke of Savoy who loved little Pierre very much, and they had scarcely arrived at Lyons before he told him that he knew he should never be able to keep him after the king had once seen him exercise in the meadow of Esnay. King Charles witnessed the wonderful evolutions he performed on his war-horse with the greatest delight; he was never weary of seeing him spur on the animal to fresh gambols; "Pique, [20] pique, encore une fois!" he cried, and all the little pages echoing the words of the king, cried in their shrill voices, "Piquez, piquez!" so that Pierre was called long after by the familiar name of "Piquet" in memory of the day.

Before the Duke of Savoy left Lyons he gave a supper to the Seigneur de Ligny and some of the chief nobles in the city. The repast was enlivened by the music of the royal minstrels and singers: it was served early, and when it was ended the company played at various games all the remainder of the evening, and drank spiced wines before they separated. This was the usual manner of entertainment at that time, and if ladies were included in the invitations, there would be dancing until midnight, which was considered a very late hour.

The years passed on, and Pierre was very happy with his companions in the house of the Seigneur de Ligny. There was then living in Burgundy a brave knight named Claude de Vauldré, whom the king summoned to Lyons, in order that the young nobles of the city might contend with him, and thus give proof of the progress they had made in their martial studies.

As soon as Claude arrived he hung up his shield, and it was a custom that if any person touched a shield thus suspended, he gave a sign that he was ready to engage in combat with its owner.

One day, as Pierre was passing by, he sighed deeply, and said to himself, "Ah, if I only knew how to equip myself for the combat, how gladly would I touch yonder shield, and so gain some real knowledge of the use of arms!" One of his comrades, Bellabre, seeing him so full of care, asked him what he was thinking about; and when he told him of his desire, and his distress at having no money to buy horses and weapons, Bellabre advised him to ask help from his uncle, the rich Abbé of Esnay.

Bayard, with hope revived by this counsel, touched the shield, and after a sleepless night set off for Esnay very early in the morning, in a little boat, with Bellabre. They found the abbé saying his matins. He grumbled terribly at first at his nephew's request, saying that the money given by the founders of the abbey was to serve God with, and not to be spent in jousts and tilting. Bayard, however, prevailed upon him to provide him with a hundred crowns and two horses; and the abbé, in a more softened mood, ordered a merchant of Lyons to furnish him with all other things that he required.

The greatest wonder was expressed in Lyons that a youth not yet eighteen years of age should venture to contend with an experienced knight like Claude Vauldré; but when the day of trial came, Bayard repelled the thrusts of his opponent in the most daring and fearless manner; and the ladies who sat in the balconies, watching the combatants in the arena below, exclaimed with one voice that he had done better than all the rest.

One morning, soon after the tournament, the Seigneur de Ligny called Pierre to him, and told him that as the war the French had long been carrying on in Italy was to be continued, he should now enter his company, which was stationed at the little town of Ayre, in Picardy. The Seigneur told him also that he would give him three hundred francs a year for his service, and three horses, richly caparisoned. Bayard then went to take leave of the king, who bestowed on him, at parting, the finest horse in his stable; and last of all, he bade farewell with many tears to the good seigneur himself, whose house had been for him a second happy home. It is worthy of remark, throughout the life of the good knight, that in whatever circumstances he was placed, he always spoke of his happiness. And what *was* the secret of that happiness, which neither the agony he endured when he lay disabled by wounds could take from him, nor the hardships and toil he had to go through during his numerous campaigns? Surely it was his loving kindness to all around him, which sprang from his own love to Almighty God and his Son Jesus Christ. To do good is truly to be happy, and love begets love. Bayard was dreaded by the enemies of his country because he was so steadfast and brave; but we never find that he had one personal enemy, or that he harboured a quarrelsome thought.

As he drew near the little town of Ayre, his future comrades rushed out on the road to meet him, they were so glad to have him amongst them, and the ladies flocked to the windows to welcome him as he passed along the streets. Bayard had sent his servant on before to prepare a great supper at his lodgings, and there he entertained his new companions the night of his arrival. And very soon after he had a tournament cried in Ayre, which lasted two days and attracted a vast concourse of people to the spot.

It was the beautiful summer time, and the little town looked very gay with the banners streaming from its windows, and the bright armour of the knights and the jewels and silken robes of the ladies flashing in the sunlight. The trumpets were sounded, and Bayard was the first to enter the lists against one of his neighbours of Dauphiné, who was a very rough man of arms. The good knight, before he vanquished him, broke his lance in five or six pieces. The trumpets sounded again in full clang, and in the next trial Bayard very nearly had his arm broken, but he won from his opponent a little casque adorned with plumes. Then came Bellabre and a formidable Scottish captain, named David Fergus, who was greatly renowned for his strength and skill.

When the first day's contest was over, there was joyous feasting and dancing in Ayre until midnight, and the next morning all the knights went to mass, after which they dined together in good fellowship, and at two o'clock in the afternoon they repaired to the arena to complete the trial. And at evening, when they had all done their part in the sport, and the air was filled with shouting and merry talking, the trumpets were sounded to command silence, and to Bayard was awarded the honour of decreeing the prizes. The young knight protested that he was not worthy of so great an honour, and was about to withdraw, but the people present insisted that he should adjudge them, and no other, because he had fought the best of all. So he gave the first prize, which was a bracelet of pure gold, to his friend Bellabre; and the second one, a fine diamond, to the gallant Scottish captain. It was usual for the knights to present the prizes they had thus won to the young maidens whom they had chosen for their brides. During the time Pierre remained in Ayre he made himself very much beloved by his liberality, and his readiness to help those who were in distress. Many of his companions were poor, although they were of noble family, and if any one of them wanted setting up in arms, or was in need of money, Bayard was sure to let him share the last crown piece he had in his purse. Besides this, he never forgot the poor, and every morning he used to attend the service of the church, which made him happy for the day, and strong to overcome evil.

When King Charles the Eighth undertook his expedition to Naples, the good knight accompanied him with the Seigneur de Ligny, and in the battle of Fornova, which the French gained over the Italians on their way back to France, he displayed great valour, and had two horses killed under him at the first charge. Whilst the French companies remained in Italy they were allowed to amuse themselves in tilting and jousts, provided no particular warfare was going on at the time; and Bayard had leisure to visit the Duchess of Savoy, at Carignan, and held a great tournament there in honour of the favourite playmate of his childhood, who was now married to Monsieur de Fluxas, an officer belonging to the household of Charles of Savoy. And here he saw many who recalled the happy days at Chambéry: it was a joyous meeting on both sides, and Bayard remembered all those who had been kind to him when he first left the old castle of Bayard, and to the master palfrenier, [21] who was very fond of him, he gave a horse worth fifty pieces of silver; and to the squire, who had been so loth to part with him in Lyons, and had now retired from the service of the Duke of Savoy, he sent a mule, because the old man was ill with the gout, and could not walk.

After the death of Charles VIII., the Italian war was continued by his successor, Louis XII., and Bayard was constantly engaged in supporting the honour of the French arms. In the year 1503 Louis declared war against Ferdinand, of Arragon, because he had behaved very badly to him by pretending to be his ally, whilst in reality he was planning to take from the French all the places they had conquered in Italy. Three great armies were prepared to invade the dominions of Ferdinand on every side. The good knight served in the first: it was composed of 18,000 infantry, and 2,000 men-at-arms, and was destined for the recovery of the kingdom of Naples, which had been wrenched out of the hands of the French by Gonsalvo, the Great Captain.

By the time the army arrived in the south of Italy, the season was far advanced, and the French and the Spaniards remained for a long time on the opposite shores of the river Garigliano, near Naples. Pedro de Paz, the leader of the Spanish troops, was a man of the most daring courage, although in person he was so small, that it is said when he was on horseback his head was all that could be seen of him above the saddle. One day he formed a plan which, had it been carried out, would have caused very great loss to the French. This was to cross the Garigliano with a hundred men-at-arms, at a place where he knew there was a ford, in the hope that the French would hasten thither to resist him, and leave his other troops to gain possession of a bridge of boats which had been thrown across the river. His plan was successful in the beginning; there was a sudden alarm in the French camp. The good knight who always liked to be where the danger was greatest, had a lodging close by the bridge; he happened to be there at the time with only one of his squires. Having heard the noise, they were just going to arm themselves, and hasten to join in the affray, when Bayard perceived 200 of the enemy's horse advancing towards the bridge. He told his companion to fly to the rest of the army and give the alarm, whilst he amused the Spaniards until succour could arrive. The good knight then went alone to the bridge with his lance in his hand, and found the Spaniards just ready to cross at the other end. But he did not let them advance, and kept the bridge single handed until his squire came back with 100 men-at-arms; the enemy thought at last his efforts could not be human! The men-at-arms, with Bayard at their head, soon forced all the Spaniards to quit their post, and chased them a good mile beyond it; they would have pursued them farther, but they saw several hundred men coming to the rescue, and they turned their horses in the direction of the camp. Bayard was always the last to retreat; on this occasion he was far behind the others, his horse being so tired that it could only go very slowly on its way; and soon a body of Spaniards bore down suddenly upon him, his horse was thrown into a ditch, and he was surrounded by twenty or thirty Spanish knights, who kept crying "Surrender, Señor, surrender!" The good knight defended himself to the utmost, but he thought he should not be able to hold out long against so many, and fortunately his comrades, who had missed him just as they had reached the bridge, were seen hastening to the spot where he was so hardly pressed.

Directly the Spaniards heard the quick tread of their horses they carried him off, and kept asking his name; but he only replied that he was a gentleman; because if they had known whom it was they had captured he might never have come out of their hands alive. A cry, however, rose on the air, "Turn, Spaniards, you shall not carry away thus the flower of chivalry!" The French came up, and a fierce struggle ensued. Bayard mounted another horse, and soon extricated himself from his enemies, exclaiming the while, "France! Bayard, whom you let go!" The Spaniards were greatly vexed and discouraged when they found out how important a prize they had lost, and began at once to retreat, while the French rode home in the winter dusk joyful and triumphant to their camp.

The good knight held out bravely against the foes of his country, but the enterprise did not succeed, and a treaty was made which obliged the French to withdraw all their forces from the kingdom of Naples, and return by sea or land to their own country. Bayard and another valiant knight named Louis d' Ars, were very indignant that such a treaty should have been made; they refused to sign it, and said they would rather stay in Italy and perish by the sword than allow the Italians to believe that all Frenchmen were cowards, and they undertook to defend several small towns which remained to the French in Naples, with a few followers who would not forsake them, and sold all their jewels and silver plate that they might be able to buy provisions and ammunition. Thus, to the astonishment of Europe, these two knights maintained the honour of their countrymen in Italy, and did not give up the towns they had engaged to defend until the following year, when the king recalled them to France, and rewarded them in proportion to their services.

The good knight was dangerously wounded some years later at the taking of Brescia. This city had opened its gates to the victorious French three years before, but had been delivered into the hands of the Venetians through the treachery of an Italian count, who resided within its walls. As soon as the king's nephew, Gaston, Duke de Nemours [22] heard of this, he marched forty leagues in the depth of winter, in the hope of recovering the town, having already sent Bayard on in advance. The day after his arrival, they took possession of the citadel, which still held out for the French, and the next day they agreed to take the town by assault. The road leading down from the citadel to the rampart was very slippery on account of the heavy rains, and the duke was obliged to take off his shoes to prevent himself from falling; still he went bravely on, followed by the good knight and his men-at-arms. When the Venetians saw Bayard at the first rampart, they tried all they could to kill him; because, they said, if he were once overcome the others would never dare approach. Bayard steadily gained his way, however, and cheered his men on to victory until he passed the rampart, and a thousand of the French were enabled to make their entrance into the town. But in doing this he received a pike-wound in his thigh; the pike going in so hard that the end of it broke, and the iron was left in the flesh. Bayard told the captain beside him that he might lead off his men now that the town was won, but that he should never pass from the place again, and reckoned himself a dead man.

The knowledge that the Chevalier was severely wounded only served to make the French captains press on the assault with greater fury, and they fought their way into the public place, or square, where they killed many of the Venetians, and obliged the others to lay down their arms. The good knight was left with two of his archers, who tried to staunch the blood that flowed from his wounds. When they saw that all the strongholds in the town were gained, they sought around until they found a wooden plank, or door, and on this they carried him into the best looking house they could see. This house belonged to an Italian gentleman, who not very courageously had fled for safety to a monastery, and had left his wife and daughters in the town. The archers knocked at the door, and were allowed to carry in their burden, and they afterwards stationed themselves outside to prevent the enemy from entering. The Italian lady received Bayard very kindly; she was grieved to see him suffering so much, and went herself with one of the archers to fetch a good surgeon to dress his wound.

It was nearly five weeks before he could rise from his bed, and during that time he had sent his *maître d'hôtel* to seek for the lady's husband, so that the whole family might live happily together under his protection, their house being the only one in Brescia that was neither sacked nor pillaged. And he said afterwards that although he had endured the greatest pain from his wound, he had never once been unhappy, because he had been with friends; it only vexed him to think that the French were getting nearer the Spaniards every day, and that a battle would soon take place, in which he would not be able to assist; and he used to tell the Duke de Nemours, who came daily to see him whilst he remained in the town, because he loved him so much, that he would rather be borne to the battle-field in a litter than not be present at all. For it was the great object of the king of France to drive the Spaniards out of Lombardy, since he knew that as long as they were roving about in Italy, his duchy of Milan would never be secure.

One day Bayard found, to his joyful surprise, that he could walk once more, and his surgeon gave him leave to start at the expiration of two days for the French camp. According to the custom of the victorious French, the whole family were in reality the prisoners of Bayard, and the Italian lady was in great trouble of mind, thinking that he would demand at least ten or twelve thousand crowns for their ransom, which was more than they were able to pay. So on the morning of the day when the good knight was to depart after dinner, she came to him, and knelt down before him. Bayard would not suffer her to kneel, so rising, she presented him with a purse which contained 1,500 ducats. When she had opened it, he laughed: "How many are there, madam?" he asked. The lady thought that he was laughing because there were so few, and began to make excuses; but when the Chevalier found out that she wanted to pay her ransom, he declared that he would take nothing from her at all; that the welcome she had given him was worth more than a hundred thousand crowns, and that he should feel himself bound in gratitude to serve her until the end of his days. It was so unusual for the French to release their prisoners without a ransom that the Italian lady was deeply moved; she went down on her knees, and kissing the hand of the good knight, she said, "Flower of chivalry, may the Lord reward you for what you have done!" She pressed him so hard however to accept the purse that Bayard consented to take it out of esteem and respect for her, and her two daughters then came to bid him farewell. The damsels were very beautiful; they were skilled in embroidery, and could sing and play the lute and spinet, and many a time the Chevalier, as he lay writhing in pain, had been cheered by their music. When they came in, they too would have knelt to thank him for his kindness and protection, but he made them rise, and dividing the ducats into three parts, he gave each of them a thousand for a marriage portion, and the five hundred that remained he gave to their mother for the relief of the religious houses in Brescia, which had been plundered by the French. The maidens now produced the parting gifts they had prepared; the Chevalier received them very graciously, and said that he should wear them as long as he lived; one was a bracelet made of gold and silver thread, and the other a purse of crimson worked in gold. Then they all touched hands after the fashion of Italy, and the good knight bade them farewell kneeling, and they all wept bitterly when he rode away from the door, they were so grieved to think they should never see him again.

When Bayard reached the camp of the Duke de Nemours, he found that his countrymen had arrived only that day before Ravenna, and that the enemy were six miles off, but the next day they came nearer by two miles. The night but one before the famous battle of Ravenna, several captains were at supper with the Duke de Nemours, talking the while of the contest which was so soon to take place. Bayard was amongst the guests, and the

Duke told him that as the Spaniards had a great respect for his talents, and were very anxious to know if he were in the camp, he thought it would be advisable for him to attempt some skirmish with them the next day, just to see how well they could fight. The good knight was delighted with the idea; "Monseigneur," he replied, "I promise you on my word of honour that, God helping, I shall see them so close before noon, that I shall be able to bring you news."

Now the Baron of Bearne, the Duke's lieutenant, coveted the glory of being the first to attack the enemy, and although the Chevalier was known to rise very early in the morning, he thought that he would rise earlier still, and thus steal a march upon him. So as soon as soon as the supper was ended, he went to tell all his followers to be ready armed before break of day, charging them also to keep the matter a profound secret.

When the good knight returned to his tent, he also arranged with some of the chief captains how the attack should be made, and then, they all went to rest until the trumpet should sound to awaken them at dawn.

It was very early the next morning when they set out, carrying with them the banners of the Duke of Lorraine unfurled, in the hope that they would bring them good luck. They did not, of course, know that the Baron of Bearne had already gone the same path; but the sound of weapons clashing, and of horses' hoofs, soon fell upon their ears; the baron had indeed crossed the canal which lay between the two armies, and had advanced to the enemy's camp; but he had been discomfited, and was forced to retire.

When Bayard saw that Neapolitans and Spaniards were boldly crossing the canal in pursuit of the fugitives, he called to his comrades to fly to the aid of their countrymen, and rushed before any into the midst of a troop of one hundred and twenty men. His comrades loved him too well not to follow him, and he chased the enemy back right into the camp, and overthrew there numbers of their tents, although the Spaniards were all astir and ready for battle. When he thought he had aroused them sufficiently, he sounded the trumpet for a retreat, and arrived in the camp of the Duke de Nemours with the news he had promised to bring him, but without having lost a single man.

The Duke now assembled all the captains and knights, and told them, that his uncle the king desired that a battle should take place at once, because he had heard that the Venetians and Swiss were about to descend into the Duchy of Milan; and it was agreed that the French army should pass the bridge of boats across the canal, and attack the enemy on the morrow.

The next morning the Duke came out of his tent at sunrise. "Look, gentlemen!" he said to his companions, "how red the sun is!" And one of them, who was much beloved by him, replied, "Do you know, Monseigneur, what that signifies? That a great captain will fall to-day: it will be either you or Cardonna, the viceroy." The duke only laughed at his remark, and went to watch the army passing the bridge with Bayard and some other knights, while the Spaniards, in great alarm, hastened to put the whole of their troops in battle array.

Just as the duke was telling the good knight, that they might fall an easy prey to their enemies, if any harquebussiers were concealed thereabouts, a body of from twenty to thirty Spaniards appeared, amongst whom was Pedro de Pas. Bayard was the first to speak. "Gentlemen," said he, "you will linger about here like ourselves until the play begins. I entreat that not a harquebuss be fired on your part, and we will not fire upon you." Pedro de Pas then asked the name of the knight who had spoken, and was overjoyed to find that he was really in the company of the Chevalier du Bayard, who had gained so much renown in Naples.

The Duke de Nemours was a merciful man, and he offered to settle the quarrel by single combat with the viceroy, to spare the effusion of blood. His followers, however, thought that the risk was too great; and the army having crossed the canal by eight o'clock in the morning, the battle began. It lasted many hours, and was very terrible on both sides; and although the Spaniards were defeated, the French bought their victory very dearly, with the life of their brave and good young prince, Gaston of Nemours. For the prediction of his friend had indeed been fulfilled, and he lay among the slain! The good knight fought all through that long battle like a hero; he had gone in pursuit of the enemy, and came back to the field late in the afternoon, to find that the duke was dead.

A short time after this, the Venetians, the Swiss, and the army sent by the Pope pressed forward, and the French were soon obliged to retire out of Lombardy, only leaving garrisons in some of the strong castles. At Pavia, Bayard made himself very famous by defending a bridge of boats, during two hours against the Swiss; he had two horses killed under him, and received a severe wound in the shoulder before he would give way. His companions thought that his wound was mortal, though he declared it was nothing, and they staunched it with moss, which they tore off the stems of trees, and with linen which they tore from their shirts. The good knight did not recover for a very long time after the French army had recrossed the mountains, and he went to his uncle the Bishop of Grenoble, in whose palace he was lodged and watched over, "like the precious stone set in pure gold." And he was so ill that he thought to his sorrow that he should die in his bed, instead of closing his eyes for ever on the battle-field; but all the people of Grenoble prayed for him—his good uncle, nobles, merchants, monks, and nuns; there was not a voice that did not rise up in prayer to the Almighty for his recovery. And after a long while his strength and spirit returned to him, and he remained some months at Grenoble, greatly honoured for all the brave deeds he had achieved.

In the battle of Guinegatte, commonly called the battle of the Spurs, from the speed with which the French soldiers took flight, the Chevalier was made prisoner, but not until he had saved his countrymen from entire disgrace by his valour. Henry the Eighth was then at war with France, and Maximilian, Emperor of Germany, was serving in the army of the English monarch for the pay of a hundred crowns a day.

Before Henry and Maximilian had arrived in the English camp, the Earl of Shrewsbury had begun the siege of Perouane, a town on the borders of Picardy, close by Guinegatte. The besieged had defended themselves bravely, and the governor of the province had succeeded in forcing his way through the English camp, to bring them a large supply of bacon and gunpowder. He had got safely back again, when the French horsemen, who had advanced to protect him, were attacked suddenly by a body of English, whilst they were straying carelessly about without their helmets and cuirasses, because they were overpowered by the intense heat of the day. Thus it was that they took flight, and that several noblemen amongst them of high rank were made prisoners. Bayard retreated with great regret; he had only fourteen men-at-arms with him, and yet he often turned back and faced his enemies. At last they came to a little bridge, where only two horsemen could pass at a time, and below it there was a deep ditch full of water. The good knight then sent word to the camp, by an archer that he had arrested the enemy for at least half an hour, and that delay, would give the army time to get into order. The archer went straight to the camp, and Bayard was left with his few men to guard the bridge. He was soon surrounded on all sides, and advised his people to surrender; and when they were all secured, he rode towards an English gentleman, who, either wearied with the fight or oppressed by the heat, was resting beneath a tree. Bayard put his sword to his throat, and exclaimed, "Surrender, man-at-arms, or you are a dead man!" The gentleman, naturally wishing to save his life, surrendered, and asked the stranger who he was. "I am the Captain Bayard," replied the knight, "and now I surrender to you, and give you my sword to hold, and entreat you to conduct me to some place of safety, and to have the kindness to let me have my sword, if we meet with any Englishmen on our way, who may desire to kill me." The gentleman promised this, and they set off for the camp of King Henry, and had really to defend themselves more than once, upon the road thither.

Bayard remained in the tent of his prisoner, who treated him well, but on the fifth day of his captivity, he said to him, "My gentleman, I wish you would lead me in safety to the camp of the king, my master, for I am utterly tired of being here."

"How?" cried the other. "We have not yet agreed as to your ransom."

"To my ransom, indeed!" said the knight; "but it is rather for me to think of yours, since you are my prisoner; and if I surrendered to you it was only to save my life. My gentleman," continued he, "whether faith is kept with me, or not, I feel assured that in some way I shall fight with you by and by."

The gentleman did not quite relish the idea of a combat with the redoubtable Bayard, so he replied in courteous terms, that he only wished to do what was right in the affair, and would consult with his captains.

When the enemy knew that Bayard was safe in the camp, they were as much pleased as if they had won another victory. The Emperor of Germany sent for him to his tent.

"Captain Bayard, my friend," said he, "I have great pleasure in seeing you. Would that I had many men like you! I think in a little while I should be able to avenge myself of all the tricks, your master has played me in times gone by." Presently, he said to him, "Methinks we have been at war together before, and I remember to have heard that Bayard was one who never fled."

"Sire," replied the Good Knight promptly, "if I had fled I should not have been here."

Then bluff King Harry came up and said, "Truly, Monsieur de Bayard, if all men were like you, the siege which I have begun before this town, would soon be raised; but any way you are my prisoner."

"Sire," answered the Chevalier, "I do not own it, and yet I would fain believe yourself and the emperor."

The gentleman whose tent Bayard had shared now appeared, and related the whole affair; and there was a discussion, as to which was really the prisoner. The Emperor, whose advice governed the movements of the English army, at last decided in favour of Bayard, but acquitted both on account of their mutual courtesy; and King Henry said that the Good Knight might leave the camp, if he would promise on his word of honour to remain unarmed for six weeks. Bayard was very grateful, both to the emperor and to the king, and went to divert himself in the country, in the best manner he could until the six weeks were passed. During this time the King of

England tried by various means, to attach him to his service, but his trouble was thrown away; it would have been impossible for the Chevalier to have entertained a disloyal thought.

Not long after this Louis the Twelfth died, and his cousin, Francis, Count of Angoulême, was declared King of France. Immediately after his coronation, the young king began to prepare secretly for the conquest of Milan, that duchy having lately returned to the allegiance of the Italian duke Sforza. Bayard was ordered to repair with three or four thousand men, to the borders of his native province of Dauphiné, and after performing several brave actions, he got down quietly into the plain of Piedmont. Prosper Colonna, the Pope's lieutenant, was there in the Castle of Carmaignolle. When he heard of the arrival of the Chevalier, he exclaimed, in a tone of extreme scorn, "That Bayard has crossed the mountains; I will take him as I would a pigeon in a cage!"

The other French captains arrived in the plain, and the Good Knight advised that they should rest their horses that night, and attack Colonna the next day at dawn in his castle.

They had a large piece of water to cross before they could get to the place; but they knew of a ford, and two or three hours after midnight they mounted their horses in silence, and set out on the road. Prosper was not alarmed, because he still thought that only Bayard was there with his company, and he would have remained at Carmaignolle, had he not received orders to change his quarters. He did not hurry himself in the least, and stopped on his journey to dine at a little town called Villefranche. When the French arrived at the castle, they found to their disappointment that Colonna was gone, and they all agreed to pursue him. The Seigneur d'Imbercourt was foremost in the troop; he soon reached the town; Colonna was already there, and his people shut the gates. The Good Knight came up in time however to gain them, and although the enemy gave the alarm to a body of three or four thousand Swiss, he made his way into the town, followed by his men-at-arms, and found the Italian commander seated at his dinner. Colonna was enraged at being thus captured, like "a pigeon in a cage" himself, instead of in battle; the Good Knight tried to cheer him up, and make the best of it, but the whole affair cost the signor, besides his liberty, 50,000 crowns worth of gold and silver plate, furniture, and money, and that was quite enough to make a man look sad. The French found a very large sum of money in the town, and nearly 700 beautiful coursers and Spanish horses.

Francis had already crossed the mountains which separate France from Italy. He was delighted to hear of the capture of Colonna, and soon waged the tremendous battle of Marignano with the Swiss, who were the partizans of Sforza and Colonna, and were indignant that Francis had succeeded in crossing the Alps. Marignano was situate about a league from the city of Milan. The Swiss were determined to defend the duchy to the last extremity, and had assembled a very large army. The battle began at four o'clock on a September afternoon in the year 1415, and was only discontinued when it was too dark to see to fight. The king passed the night in his armour on the carriage of a cannon, and was surprised at daybreak to find the enemy within a few paces of him in readiness to renew the attack. The young king and the chevalier fought at Marignano side by side, and both displayed extraordinary valour; and when the victory was decided for the French, Francis, to reward Bayard for the great share he had had in it, received the honour of knighthood from his hands.

The day of Marignano, "the combat of giants," as an old Italian hero called it, who had been in eighteen pitched battles, was disastrous indeed for the Swiss, for it is said that when they began to retreat they left 10,000 of their comrades lying dead upon the battle-field.

In the last charge that was made, Bayard was mounted on a fiery courser, the first he had ridden having been killed under him. He was so closely beset that the bridle was torn from his horse, and the animal, thus freed from restraint, galloped off and made its way through the enemy's ranks; it would have carried its rider right into the midst of a troop of Swiss, if its course had not been intercepted by a field full of vines entwined from tree to tree; the good knight but for this timely wall of defence, must assuredly have fallen into the hands of his enemies. He had not quite lost his senses in the rapid flight, and he glided down gently from his horse, threw away his arms and a part of his armour, and crawled along a ditch, in the direction as he supposed of the French camp. Fortunately he was not mistaken; he soon had the delight of hearing the cry of "France! France!" in the distance, and was enabled to reach his companions, and rejoice with them over the great victory they had gained; although a victory bought with the lives of so many fellow creatures, cannot but bring a sharp pang of sorrow to the heart of every man.

The fame of Bayard had now risen to such a height, that nearly all the young nobles of France, begged to be allowed the honour of serving under him, in the defence of the town of Mezieres. Maximilian and Ferdinand were both dead, and Charles V. was Emperor of Germany and King of Spain. Charles, who was quite as ambitious as the young king of France, had ordered the Count of Nassau to advance towards the frontiers, and lay siege to the town of Mousson. The men who defended it were cowards, and lay down their arms almost without fighting. The Count, finding this success so easy, next besieged Mezieres, and through this town the Emperor intended his troops to have passed into France. But Francis knew that if he suffered Mezieres to be taken, it would be the most foolish thing he could do; it was like giving the enemy the key of the gate that kept them out of France. So he wisely ordered Bayard to hasten to its defence; and although the Good Knight had only 1,000 men in the place, he obliged the Count of Nassau, and his 35,000 Germans, to retire with shame and loss after a lengthened siege. The service he thus performed for his country was very great, and the king rewarded him for it with a hundred lances, and the collar of St. Michael.

In the year 1524 he was sent into Italy to oppose the army of the Constable de Bourbon, who had left his own king to serve the Emperor. Bourbon was led to do this, on account of the many affronts he had received from the beautiful and haughty Louisa, of Savoy, the mother of Francis I.; still, however great the cause of offence may be, it is quite inexcusable for a man to bear arms against his country.

The chief command of the army was given to Bonnivet: he was very brave, but so rash that his zeal often did more harm than good, and he was totally wanting in the judgment, and presence of mind a great captain ought to possess. Lannoy, the viceroy of Naples, had collected a large number of troops; to these were added the forces of the Marquis of Pescara, the general of the Spaniards, and those of the traitor Bourbon. Bonnivet failed in his plan of attack, and was obliged to try and get back into France by crossing the valley of Aosta; but on his way he received a bad wound in the arm, and could no longer lead on his men. In his distress he sent word to Bayard that he alone could save the French army if he would. The good knight had thought the whole enterprise ill-judged, and when he set out at the head of his men-at-arms, he had not been cheerful and hopeful as he had been accustomed to be whenever he entered on a fresh campaign. Nevertheless he swore in reply to Bonnivet that he would either save the army or perish in the attempt; and as he had always courted the post of danger, he took the command of the rear, and made his men try bravely like himself to sustain the whole shock of the enemy's troops, whilst the rest of the army gained time to effect a retreat. This was at a place near Romagnano. As Bayard was thus striving he was wounded by a musket-ball, and the shock was so great that he uttered the word "Jesus," and then said that it was all over with him on earth. Faint from pain and loss of blood, he held on as long as he could to the bow of his saddle, but sank at last to the ground, and desired to be placed under a tree with his face turned towards the foe. And there the good knight lifted up the hilt of his sword, and kissed it as though it had been the cross, and saying, softly, "Miserere mei, Deus!" lay back pale and calm to wait for the approach of death. His faithful *maître d'hôtel*, who had followed him through many dangers, was with him now, and was almost beside himself with grief.

"Jacques, my friend," said the dying knight, "do not mourn for me. It is the will of God that I should quit this world where I have ever received a full measure of His grace, and far more honour than I deserved. The only regret I have in dying is, that I have not done all that I ought to have done, and if I had lived longer, I would have hoped to have made amends for my past faults. But as it is, I implore my Maker to have mercy upon my poor soul, and trust through his great and boundless love that he will not judge me with rigour; feeling assured that Thou, oh my Saviour, hast promised pardon to all those who turn to Thee with humble and contrite hearts."

In this condition he was found by the Constable de Bourbon, who spoke to him thus; "Monsieur de Bayard, truly I pity you."

"Ah, Monsieur," replied the chevalier, "do not pity me, but rather have compassion on yourself for having fought against your king, your country, and your oath."

The Marquis of Pescara came by soon after, and was deeply grieved to see him in such a state; he ordered a tent to be pitched over him, and had him tended with the utmost care, but it was of no avail; a mortal blow had been struck, and the good knight rendered up his soul to God, as so many of his ancestors had done, upon the battle-field.

Pescara had his body embalmed and conveyed to his kinsmen in Dauphiné, and the Duke of Savoy decreed that royal honours should be paid to it on its mournful journey. When it reached Dauphiné, people of all ranks came out to meet it, and then returned to their houses and shut themselves up in sorrow and gloom. The body was interred at Minimes, in a church founded by the Bishop of Grenoble.

There was mourning throughout many lands when it was known that the Good Knight was dead. King Francis was very much attached to him, and could not get over the loss he had sustained for a very long time. And the following year, when he had been obliged to surrender to Lannoy after the battle of Pavia, he exclaimed sadly within his prison walls, "Ah, Bayard, if thou hadst been alive, I should not have been here!"

Thus had the Chevalier lived, faithful to the promise of his childhood; ever ready to risk his life in the service of his country, helpful and loving to all, joyous and light-hearted. When he was in the enemy's territory he strictly defrayed every expense he incurred, and very often left some kind remembrance for those who had served him: in success he showed mercy, and made himself as much beloved by the vanquished as by his own soldiers. He never wished for the highest place or envied the good fortune of other men. Amid the spoils of war he seemed to desire nothing for himself, and one instance alone will suffice to show how far he was removed from any selfish feelings. During the war with the Spaniards, he received notice one day that a large sum of money was on its way to the Spanish commander. His own troops being in great want of necessaries he resolved to obtain this money, which was fair to do in warfare; so he sent some of his men to waylay the bearers of it in one part of the country, while his companion Tardien watched for it in another. Bayard had the good luck to seize the treasure, and found it to consist of 15,000 ducats. The Spaniard who carried it was in great terror at having fallen into the hands of the enemy, and gave it up without a murmur. Tardien was brave and merry-hearted, but he had the misfortune of being very poor, and he was terribly grieved on his return to the camp to find that he had not been the happy man to secure the money, and declared that the half of the sum would have redeemed his fortunes for ever.

Bayard was in a cheerful mood, and he asked his soldiers how much of the treasure they thought Tardien ought to receive. They replied, "None at all." Then Bayard, after enjoying for a time the dismay of his companion in arms, called him to him, and gave him 7,500 ducats, the exact half of the sum they had captured. The Good Knight then divided the remainder amongst his soldiers, not keeping one farthing for himself, and sent the Spaniard with an escort to a place of safety whence he could return to his own home.

FOOTNOTES:

[20] "Piquer," an old French word, signifying "to spur on, to animate, or encourage."

[21] *Palfrenier*, "groom of the stables."

[22] Gaston was Governor of Milan.

SIR MARTIN FROBISHER

One summer's day, in the year 1576, Queen Elizabeth stood at the window of her palace at Greenwich, waving her hand in sign of farewell as two small barks and a pinnace glided gently down the river Thames. The barks were the *Gabriel* and the *Michael*. On board the first one was the gallant Martin Frobisher, who, after having waited fifteen years for funds to enable him to carry out his voyage, was now on his way in search of a north-west passage to China. Little is known of the early days of Frobisher, except that he was at Doncaster, in Yorkshire, and that he was well skilled in maritime knowledge, and one of the most experienced seamen of his time. The passage he proposed to find, he thought would enable his countrymen to reach the shores of China in far less time than by sailing as the Portuguese always sailed, all round by the Cape of Good Hope; and thus for years before he had started, he had been going from friend to friend, nobleman and merchant, in the hope of finding some one to help him to get together a fleet. At last he found a patron in Ambrose Dudley, the good Earl of Warwick, and with his help, and his own untiring efforts besides, he raised sufficient money to fit out the two vessels and the one small pinnace, which had provisions on board to last twelve months.

After the little fleet had gone past the palace, Queen Elizabeth sent one of the gentlemen of her court on board the *Gabriel* to tell Frobisher how much pleasure the enterprise afforded her, and to bid him come and take leave of her the following day. She was proud, too, to think that one of her subjects was brave enough to venture up into the icy seas and cold regions, the very idea of which had struck terror into the hearts of many a mariner, when he had met on the ocean great icebergs floating southwards, as though they were messengers sent to warn him of approaching the frozen seas.

When Frobisher had got as far as the Shetland Isles, he turned his course towards the west, and on the 11th of July, nearly four weeks after he had started, he came in sight of land, which he supposed to be the Freeseland seen by a Venetian, named Zeno, two hundred years before. He could not land there because of the great blocks of ice which filled the sea near the shore, and they had much ado to keep clear of them, because there was a thick fog. Here a great misfortune happened; the pinnace disappeared in the mist, and the services of the four men it had on board were thus lost. The company of the *Michael* also began to distrust the voyage, and to repent that they had engaged in it. Under cover of the fog, they went off towards England, and were so wicked as to say on their arrival that the bark *Gabriel* had been cast away.

Thus forsaken, the brave captain went on alone; the mast of his vessel was broken, and the topmast was blown over; nevertheless he continued to sail towards the north-west, thinking that he must surely come to some shore. And nine days after he had seen Freeseland, he came to a high piece of land, which he called Queen Elizabeth's; it was part of what is now called Labrador. Still more to the north he reached another foreland, with a great bay or passage of sea dividing two lands, but this was so blocked up with ice that he had to wait until it melted, or was carried away by currents. He called the passage "Frobisher's Straits," after himself, by which name it has been known ever since. If any little readers will unfold a map of North America and look just north of Hudson's Straits, they will see Frobisher's Straits, and how the land on either side is broken up into islands, some of which are named "Hall's Islands," after Christopher Hall, the master of the bark *Gabriel*. Frobisher thought as yet that the shores were all firm land; and when the ice broke up, he sailed sixty leagues along the strait, and there he landed. First of all he had to defend himself from some great deer, which ran at him in such a manner that he had a very narrow escape of his life. Another time when he landed he went to the top of a hill, and saw from thence several objects in the distance which he thought were porpoises or seals, but when they came nearer he found that they were boats filled with men. The boats were made of sealskins, with a keel of wood inside. The men were of dark complexion, with long black hair, broad faces, and flat noses; the women's faces were painted in blue streaks. Some of these people hid behind a rock, and were evidently watching for an opportunity of stealing his boat, but he hastened down the hill just in time to secure it, and went back to the vessel. It was terribly cold already; in one night the snow lay a foot thick upon the hatches: the brief summer of the northern regions was past. The natives soon began to come on board the bark, and to talk with the sailors in an unknown tongue; they brought the captain salmon and flesh which they eat raw themselves; also bearskins and sealskins, for which Frobisher gave them toys, bells, and looking-glasses. They got very friendly with his men, although he warned them not to trust them too quickly; and one day five of the sailors were enticed by the savages to go in a boat to the shore, and neither men nor boat ever appeared again. What was to be done? Frobisher was on board his bark, and now the only boat was gone, and he could not get to the shore. He thought that he must try and capture one of the sealskin boats of the natives, and he rang a low, sweet-toned bell, which was sure to be a great temptation to the wild men, and made signs that he would give it to him who should fetch it. The first bell he purposely threw into the sea, and then he rang another. The savages, getting more eager to secure the prize, crowded around him, and one came so very near that he had just put out his hand to grasp the bell, when the captain pulled him, boat and all, on board the bark. The poor savage was said to have been so angry at being captured, that he bit his tongue in two in his rage; he was brought to England as a specimen of the newly found race, but he fell ill soon after his arrival and died.

As the cold was rapidly increasing, Frobisher began to think of returning home to report what he had seen, and after many useless attempts to land, on account of the ice along the coasts, he told his men when next they could set foot on shore, that they were to bring him whatever they could find in memory of the region he had taken possession of in the queen's name. Some of them brought him a few flowers, some only grasses, and one brought him a piece of black stone very like sea-coal, which from its weight seemed to be a mineral. Frobisher did not think much of it at first sight, but he brought it with him to England. He arrived in his native country on the 2nd day of October, and all people praised him for his courage and perseverance; and it was thought that if another expedition were made, there would be every chance of finding the desired north-west passage to China.

One day when he was with some friends in London, it happened that he had nothing to show for his voyage except the lump of coal. The wife of one of the adventurers who was present, threw by chance a piece of it into the fire, and it burned so long that at last it was taken out and quenched in a little vinegar, when lo! as if by magic, it appeared "like a bright marquisset" of gold. It was then shown to some gold finers in London, who tried it and found that it contained pure gold, and gave great hope that more might be found in the region whence it was brought. The gold finers even offered themselves to share in a fresh enterprise, so that a second voyage was proposed for the following year, Queen Elizabeth herself entering heartily into the scheme.

The second expedition was fitted out in a more important manner than the first one had been. Frobisher sailed in a tall ship of the queen's, which was called the *Aid*, accompanied by the two barks *Michael* and *Gabriel*. The vessels were provisioned for six months, and had on board in all 140 men, although many more would have liked to go on the voyage.

They sailed northwards until they anchored in the bay of St. Magnus, one of the Orkney Isles. The inhabitants fled in terror as soon as the ship's company landed, and only took heart when they heard for what purpose they had come. For few indeed were the visitors who came to those barren islands, except perhaps the pirates who roamed the northern seas. There is scarcely a tree amongst the whole group, and the people, having no wood, make their fires of turf and heather to cheer them during the long stormy winter. But the nights in these cold northern latitudes are made bright and beautiful by the aurora borealis, which flashes across the sky, and is of the same nature as lightning, only that it travels through a higher region of the air. Sometimes it is purple and sometimes green, and where the air is driest it is red. When the auroræ, or northern lights, flicker in the sky, the inhabitants of the Shetland Isles call them, "the merry dancers."

The gold finers were very glad that they stopped on their way at the Orkneys, for in one of the islands they found a mine of silver. The vessels only stayed there one day, however, and then put out to sea, now drifting to the north and now to the west, as the wind shifted. They were seventy-six days without sight of land, but they met on their way trunks of trees, and monstrous fishes and fowls. At length the wind was prosperous, and they came to Greenland, where the sea near the coast was again full of drift ice. One day whilst they were cruising about here they dropped a hook into the sea, and caught an enormous fish called a halibut, which is said to have furnished a whole day's food for the ship's company. It must have been a very large fish to have dined and supped 140 persons. All along the dreary shores the only living creatures they saw were some little birds. The weather, being very cold and stormy they made for Frobisher's Straits, and came again to the smaller of Hall's Islands, where the ore had been taken up the year before, but they only found this time one little piece. On the large island, however, they found plenty of what they supposed to be gold, and Frobisher, with forty gentlemen and soldiers, ascended a steep hill, and planting a column or cross upon it, he sounded a trumpet, and called the place Mount Warwick, after the good earl. Then they knelt down in a ring, and said their prayers and thanksgivings. As they were going back to their boats, they saw a number of savages making signs to them from the top of the hill, as if they wished to be friendly, but Frobisher, remembering the fate of the five mariners, did not feel inclined to trust them, and he only held up two of his fingers to signify that two of their men should advance towards two of his own. This was done, and then they began to be more confident of each other's designs. The people here had a very odd way of bartering their wares: they would bring sealskins and raw flesh and lay them on the ground, and make signs that the strangers should do the same with the things they meant to exchange. Then they went away, and if they liked the toys and the beads they saw on the ground, they came back in a little while and took them up, leaving their own wares behind them; and if they did not like them, they gathered up their property and departed.

After passing through many dangers and tempests Frobisher found a bay which he thought would be a good harbour for his ships, and he landed with his gold finers on a little island, where all the sands and cliffs glittered so brightly, that they thought they had indeed come to a land of gold. But when they tried it, to their great disappointment it turned out to be only black-lead. In the same sound they came to a small island, to which they gave the name of Smith's Island, because the smith belonging to the ship's company first set up his forge there. Here they found a mine of silver, but they had a great deal of trouble to get it out of the rocks.

Soon after this Frobisher marched upon the southern shore of the strait in search of ore with all his best men, and when he had appointed leaders, and told all those who were to follow them that they must be orderly and persevering, he made every man kneel down and thank God that He had preserved them hitherto from all dangers. Then, with a banner flying, they marched towards the tops of the mountains, which were steep and very difficult to ascend. The whole land was silent; not a human being was to be seen, so they went back to their ships, and landed next on the northern shore. Here they saw people, and found hidden under a stone such things as kettles made of fish-skins, knives of bone, and bridles. One of the savages took a bridle and caught with it a dog belonging to the strangers, to show how dogs were used to draw the sledges.

Five leagues from Bear's Sound, Frobisher found a bay in which he could anchor, near a small island, which he named after the Countess of Warwick, and this was the farthest place he visited that year. There was plenty of ore in it, and Frobisher set the miners to work, and worked hard himself also, that he might encourage the others by his example. And he sent the bark *Michael*, in which he had come to the island, for the *Aid* and the rest of his people. They were very much astonished to see on the mainland the dwellings of the Esquimaux; these were holes in the ground, shaped like an oven, and were usually made at the foot of a hill for shelter, and opened towards the south. Above ground they built with whalebone, because they had no timber, and covered in the roof of it with sealskins, and strewed moss on the floor for a carpet. Travellers of more recent date describe the huts of the Esquimaux, as the people in these northern regions were called, as being made in the same manner. A winter hut is a hole hollowed out in the earth or snow, like a cellar; a large piece of ice serves for a door, and a lamp burns inside, where the family sleep on the skins of seals and sea-dogs. Close by is a similar hole, where they eat the flesh of whales, seals, and sea-dogs—and all of it raw. The mariners who went with Frobisher tell how the savages ate ice when they were thirsty, and could get no water. Their dogs were not unlike wolves, and were yoked together to draw the sledges; the smaller ones they fattened and kept for eating. Their weapons were made of bone, and their bow-strings of sinews; they clothed themselves in the skins of seals and sea-dogs, and sometimes even in garments made of feathers; for God, in His loving mercy, has given the fowls thicker feathers than those of more southern latitudes, and the animals warmer furs for the comfort of man, just as He has given luscious fruits to refresh his parched lips in tropical countries, and gigantic trees to shelter him from the intense heat of the sun.

A captive, who had been taken by some of the mariners, was shown a portrait of the savage who had been enticed on board the *Gabriel* the year before. When he saw it, he began talking to it, and asking it questions, just as if it had been really alive. He told the strangers by signs that he had knowledge of the five men who were missing, and declared that they had not been eaten up by the savages. It is supposed that they lived the rest of their lives amongst the savages; and Frobisher determined, as he could find no trace of them, that he would load his ships with the ore he had found, and return to England. He was very proud when all the labour was brought to an end, for with "five poor miners," and a few gentlemen and soldiers, they had carried on board almost two hundred tons of ore in twenty days. On the night of the 21st of August the whole company were ready to embark, and glad they were to return, for they were very weary, and the water began to freeze around their ships at night. The next day they took down their tents, lighted bonfires on the highest hill, and having marched round the island with their banner unfurled, they fired a volley of cannon in sign of farewell, and after having encountered several storms on their voyage, they reached Milford Haven about the end of September.

When Frobisher arrived in England he hastened to Windsor, where he was very graciously received by Queen Elizabeth. A third expedition was planned for the next spring, both to search for gold and to try and discover the north-west passage. A strong fort was devised, the pieces of which were to be carried in one of the ships, and put together when they arrived in the new region, to which Queen Elizabeth gave the name of "Meta Incognita," or "Unknown Land." The fort was intended for the people to dwell in, who were to remain there during the winter, whilst twelve of the vessels out of the fifteen that composed the fleet were to come home laden with ore—that is to say, if it were to be found. All the captains bade the queen farewell at Greenwich, and kissed her hand, and she gave to Frobisher "a chain of fair gold," to show the delight she took in his enterprise. They left Harwich for the third time on the 31st of May—Frobisher sailed in the *Aid*: the strictest order was to be observed during the voyage; the whole company on board were to serve God twice a day with the prayers of the Church of England: the sailors were not allowed to swear, or to play at cards and dice. Every evening all the fleet had to come up and speak with the admiral, and the watchword, if any came up in the night, was this, "Before the world was God." And the answer from the other vessel was, "After God, came Jesus Christ His Son."

On the 20th of June, after having sailed fourteen days without sight of land, they came, at two o'clock in the morning, to the west of Freeseland. Frobisher took possession of it in the queen's name, calling it West England, and gave the name of Charing Cross to one of its high cliffs. The nights in the northern regions are never dark during the summer months. As far north as the vessels sailed the sun does not set until after ten o'clock, and it rises again before two, so that a great part of the night, the sky is filled with the rosy flush of sunrise and sunset. Then, in the winter, when the days are as short as the nights are in summer, because the north part of the world is turned away from the sun, the moon and stars are wondrously bright, and with the northern lights enliven the long dark hours.

The savages in West Freeseland were like those in Meta Incognita; they were very timid, and fled at the approach of the strangers, leaving all their household goods behind them. Amongst these the mariners found some dried herrings and a box of small nails, also some pieces of carved fir wood; but for whatever they took they left pins, knives, or looking-glasses in exchange.

From Freeseland they went towards Frobisher's Straits, and on the way one of the ships, called the *Salamander*, struck a great whale such a blow with her stern that she stood quite still. A horrible noise rose up from the sea, and the next day the dead body of a whale was seen floating about.

One night the vessels entered somewhere inside the straits, and found the whole place frozen into "walls, bulwarks, and mountains," which they could not pass: they had to stem and strike the rocks of ice to make their way at all. Some of the fleet, where they found the sea open, entered in, and were in great danger.

The bark *Dennis* struck against one of the rocks and sank within sight of the fleet. In her distress she fired a gun, and happily the whole of her crew were rescued in the boats that were sent to her aid. It was a great misfortune, nevertheless, because part of the fort was on board, and was thus lost. A violent wind from the south-east drove the ice on the backs of the vessels. The mariners and miners had never witnessed such peril before, and they were indeed in terrible plight, because they were shut in by blocks of ice on all sides, and had to fix cables, beds, and planks around their ships to protect them from them, or they would have been all cut to pieces. Besides this they had to stand the whole night and the next day beating it off with poles, pikes, and oars—Frobisher working hardest of all, and cheering his men by his kind words, and his brave, steadfast spirit. And those who were not strong enough to work prayed for the rest; which the weak can always do, whilst stronger men are doing God's will by helping their fellow-creatures; and prayer and work, blended in one, rise up an acceptable offering to the Father in heaven.

Four of the vessels were out in the open sea, and during the storm the mariners were in great alarm for the safety of those shut up in the ice, and they too knelt praying for them around their mainmast. The wind at last blew from the north-west, and dispersed the ice, and the second night the ships in distress were seen of the four others. Then the whole fleet veered off seaward, meaning to wait until the sun should melt the icebergs, or the winds drive them quite away, and when they had got out far into the sea, they took in their sails and lay adrift. On the 7th of July they thought they saw the North Foreland of the straits, but there was a dense fog at the time; and the snow often fell in flakes so that they could not clearly see, although now and then the sun would shine on the vessels with intense heat. Thus they were carried far out of the way, and the lands in that region were so much alike that Frobisher took counsel with the captains of the fleet, to determine what part they had reached.

The fogs lasted twenty days, and during that time they had indeed drifted sixty leagues out of their way into unknown straits. Frobisher was very anxious to recover the position he had lost, and as soon as he saw the ice a little open he bravely led the way and anchored at last in the Countess of Warwick's Sound. Just as he thought all peril was past, he met a great iceberg, which forced the anchor through the ship's bows and made a breach. Here they found, to their joy, two barks, which had been missing since the night of their greatest danger: it was a joyful meeting, and a good man, named Master Wolfall, who had left his living in his own country, and his wife and children, in the hope of converting the heathens in the new land, preached a sermon to the whole company, in which he told them to thank God for their deliverance, and reminded them that they should ever watch and pray, since none could tell how soon he might die.

Now that they were all assembled once more Frobisher lost no time, but set at work at once to look for the ore. Gentlemen and soldiers, all helped the miners in their labour, whilst the captains of the vessels sought out new mines, and the gold finers made trial of the ore. But when they wanted to raise the fort, so many parts of it had been destroyed in the storm that it was no longer fitted for its object, and although one of the brave captains wanted to remain there with only fifty men, it was found that a building large enough to hold them all could not be raised before the winter set in. The cold was now rapidly increasing; every night the ships' ropes were frozen so that no man might handle them without cutting his hands; besides this the vessels were leaky, and the ice at any moment might have blocked them in altogether, when all on board must have perished.

Thus Frobisher was compelled to return to England without having found the passage he had hoped all his life to discover. It is said that if he had not had charge of the fleet, he would have sailed straight to the South Sea, and thus pointed out a nearer route to China.

Before they left, they caused a house of lime and stone to be built, on the Countess of Warwick's Island, which they hoped would remain standing until the following year, and they left in it bells, pictures, looking-glasses, whistles, and pipes for the delight of the savages, and an oven, with bread baked in it, that they might taste it and see how it was made. Then they sowed peas and corn, and various sorts of grain, to see if they would grow, and they buried all the timber left of the fort, that it might be ready for them to use if they came to the place again.

Whilst the ships were being laden with the ore, the admiral wanted to find something else, and he went higher up the straits in a pinnace. It was then that he discovered that the land on either side was not all firm as he had imagined, but broken up into many islands.

On the voyage home some of the vessels got scattered during the violent storms that arose, and they were kept long apart, but they all reached England by October of the year 1578.

After this there is no account of Frobisher until he went in his ship the *Aid* on an expedition to the West Indies with Sir Francis Drake, and was present at the taking and sacking of St. Domingo. When Philip II. of Spain sent the Invincible Armada to invade England, the English fleet prepared to resist it was divided into four squadrons, and Frobisher commanded one of them in the ship called the *Triumph*. Lord Howard of Effingham, the Lord High Admiral of the fleet, was a witness of his gallant conduct on that occasion, and knighted him on board the *Triumph* whilst the action was going on. A little later he served under Sir Walter Raleigh in an expedition directed towards the coasts of Spain. And in 1594 Queen Elizabeth, having engaged to help King Henry the Fourth of France against the Spaniards, he was sent with four vessels to protect the coasts of Normandy and Bretagne from their attacks.

On being told that they had seized the Fort of Croysson, near Brest in Bretagne, and that Sir John Norris was trying to regain it, he hastened to land his troops and join the English and French. With the help he afforded the fort was taken; and although he was wounded severely during the assault, he brought back the fleet in safety to Plymouth.

Soon after he arrived, however, his wound proved mortal, through the carelessness, as it is said, of his surgeon, and England lost the services of one of her bravest and most faithful officers. His chroniclers say of him that he was courageous, clever, upright, hasty, and severe. He was not the less a hero because he did not succeed in his undertakings; his attempts were made in an earnest and faithful spirit, and his example served to encourage other men to embark in fresh voyages of discovery, which proved more fortunate than his own.

It is said that some of the ore he brought home the third time did not prove to be gold, and Queen Elizabeth therefore renounced the idea of a fourth expedition.

In her wardrobe of jewels she preserved the bone of a strange fish, "like a sea-unicorn," the mariners had found on their second voyage, embedded in the ice. "The fish was twelve yards long," round like a porpoise, with a bone of two yards growing out of the snout or nostrils.

SIR WALTER RALEIGH

Sir Walter Raleigh, famed as a soldier, a sailor, an author, and a courtier, was born in Devonshire, in the year 1552. His father, Walter Raleigh, whose ancestors were known before the Conquest, had an estate near Plymouth; his mother was Elizabeth, daughter of Sir Philip Camperdown. He received the earlier part of his education at a school in the parish of Budely; at the age of sixteen we find that he was a commoner at Oxford, and already distinguished as an orator and a philosopher. A year later he went as a volunteer with one of his relations to help the Protestants in France, and afterwards served in the Netherlands under the Prince of Orange.

Raleigh had naturally a very active mind, and when he was not engaged in war, he would be busily employed in planning expeditions to the New World, some of which were carried out partly at his own expense. He had read the voyages of Columbus and of Vasco de Gama with the deepest interest, and, like many other ardent men of his time, desired earnestly to follow in the path of those brave pioneers.

In the year 1580 he commanded the royal troops in Ireland at the time of Desmond's rebellion. Philip II., to punish Elizabeth for having helped his Flemish subjects, sent a number of Spaniards and Italians to join the rebels. The Spanish general was besieged in a fort he had built at Kerry; he was forced to surrender, and the enemies of Raleigh cast great blame on him for the cruelties exercised towards the unhappy prisoners, whilst in reality he was only carrying out the orders of Lord Grey, the deputy of Ireland.

In a dispute he had with Lord Grey on his return to England, Raleigh defended himself so cleverly, that he drew upon him the attention of the queen; and an incident which occurred about this time served to bring him into great favour at court.

The queen was out walking with some of her courtiers, and having come to a muddy place, she paused, as if in doubt whether to cross it or not. Raleigh was present, and he immediately threw off a beautiful new cloak he wore, and spread it on the ground. The queen tripped lightly over it, much pleased with the gallant action, which she never forgot.

Raleigh was of middle height; he had dark hair, and was said to have been very handsome, although he had an exceedingly high forehead, and was "long-faced and sour-lidded." His dress as he stood amongst the courtiers would have consisted of a doublet of silk or satin fitting closely to the body, with enormous silken or velvet hose, richly ornamented; a peaked hat, and the cloak of gay hue, "fronted with gold and silver lace," would have completed the costume. Raleigh was always richly attired; at one time of his life he had a suit of armour composed of solid plates of silver, with which he wore a belt adorned with precious stones; and Sir Walter Scott describes a portrait he had seen of him which represented him clad in white satin, with a chain of very large pearls hanging around his neck.

The queen in the course of time bestowed on him lands in Ireland, both in the counties of Cork and Waterford. She also gave him an estate at Sherborne, in Dorsetshire, where he laid out some beautiful gardens. He asked so many favours for his friends, as well as for himself, that Elizabeth once said to him soon after she had knighted him, "When shall you cease to be a beggar, Sir Walter?"

"When your Majesty ceases to be benevolent," he replied.

The court life, however gay and pleasant, did not satisfy his eager spirit, and he rejoiced very much when the queen granted him a patent for the discovery and planting of new lands in America. For this purpose he fitted out two small vessels, which reached the coast of Florida in the year 1585. They sailed northward as far as an island called Roanoke, and found a tract of land on the continent, to which Elizabeth gave the name of Virginia, but it did not really become a flourishing colony until the reign of her successor.

Raleigh, like many other noble-minded men of his time, bore a great hatred to Spain on account of her tyrannies; and when the invincible Armada came to invade England, he was amongst the bravest of those who fought for their queen and their country. And the next year he held an important command under Drake and Norris in an expedition to place Don Antonio on the throne of Portugal.

When he returned to England, after having won great fame by his valour, he found that the young Earl of Essex was rising rapidly in the queen's favour. Much jealousy existed between these two courtiers; they were constantly quarrelling, and the following incident will show how petty were the means used by Essex to annoy his rival.

The nobles used to make a very splendid appearance at the jousts and tournaments which were held on the queen's birthday, and on one of these occasions Raleigh took it into his head to accoutre all his followers in orange-coloured plumes. Essex hearing of this, got together a much more numerous cavalcade, decked all in the colour chosen by Raleigh, and appeared at the head of his followers dressed in a complete suit of orange-colour, so that when he entered the tilt-yard in sight of Elizabeth, the followers of his rival only looked "like so many appendages to his own train." [23] Raleigh once set out at the head of a fleet with two of the queen's ships, and had the good fortune to capture a Portuguese vessel which had a very rich cargo. It was in the year 1595 that he sailed with five vessels for the discovery and conquest of Guiana, [24] a country of South America, which was called "El Dorado," on account of the gold mines it was supposed to contain. This was an enterprise he had planned during some months that he had been living in retirement at Sherborne, having incurred the displeasure of the queen. First of all he had sent out a captain to the spot, who made a favourable report of his voyage when he returned home. So Raleigh put out to sea and landed in the island of Trinidad, where he burnt the fort of Saint Joseph, which had been lately constructed by the Spaniards, and took Don Antonio, the Spanish governor, prisoner. He treated Antonio very kindly, and gained from him some valuable information in reference to the country he desired to explore. He was now very eager to set out on his enterprise, and liked the idea of it all the better because it would undoubtedly be attended with danger. He left his ships at Cariapan, in Trinidad, and sailed with a hundred men in several small barks to find "the golden land." And before he returned to England he had sailed 400 miles up the river Orinoco, which flows through Guiana, thus being the first Englishman who had ventured in that direction.

Sir Walter Raleigh wrote some strange accounts of the people he found in the new country. Those that inhabited the mouth of the Orinoco upon the northern branches of the river were called "Tissitinas;" they were very brave, and talked slowly and sensibly. In dry weather they had their dwellings on the ground like most other people, but between May and September the Orinoco rising thirty feet and overflowing the broken land, they lived up in the trees, as Columbus had already found men living in other parts a century before. They never eat anything that was planted or sown, and for bread they used the tops of the palmitos. [25] The people dwelling on the branches of the Orinoco called Capuri, and Macureo, were skilful makers of canoes, and sold them for gold and tobacco. When their chief, or king, died, they had the strange custom of keeping his body until all the flesh fell off its bones, and then they adorned the skull with gay-coloured feathers, and the limbs with gold plates, and hung up the skeleton in the house the chief had dwelt in when alive. The more gentle natives used to make war on the cannibals, but all tribes were at peace with one another, and held the Spaniards for their common enemy when the English appeared amongst them.

Sometimes the adventurers suffered greatly from thirst and from the excessive heat of the climate, since Guiana lies all in the torrid zone, the hottest part of the earth. In one district they passed through, which was low and marshy, the water that issued out of the boggy ground was almost red, and they could only fill their waterpots with it about noon, for if they filled them at morning or evening, it was as bad to drink as poison, and at night it was worst of all. The wine that was used in some parts was very strong; it was made of the juice of different fruits and herbs, and highly seasoned with pepper. The natives kept it in great earthen pots, which held ten or twelve gallons each.

At one time during their travels the weather became fearfully hot. The rivers were bordered with high trees, which met overhead and shut out the air, so that they panted for breath; the currents were against them; the water was very unwholesome to drink, and their bread was all gone. They lived on fish, and the fruits they plucked along the banks of the rivers. The beautiful flowers of the tropics twined around the great trees in the shade, and there were birds flitting about, as Sir Walter writes, "crimson, carnation, orange, tawny, and purple!" Still, they were in great want of bread, and an old native pilot whom they had taken, promised them that if they would enter a branch of the river on their right hand, with only their barge and wherries, and leave the galley they had come in to anchor in the great river, he would take them to a town, where they would find bread and poultry. So they set off in their wherries, and, because they thought the place was so near, they took no food with them at all. The day wore on, and still the pilot said "a little farther," until the sun was low in the sky, and they had glided down the stream forty miles. Then all at once it became dark, because there is no twilight in the tropics; dark as pitch, they said; the river narrowed and the trees bent over it so closely, that they had to cut their passage through the branches with their swords. They distrusted the pilot, although the poor old man, who must have been somewhat out of his reckoning, still kept assuring them that they had only a little further to go; and an hour after midnight, to their great joy they saw a light, and heard the barking of dogs, and came to a village or town which was almost empty, because nearly all its inhabitants had gone to the head of the Orinoco to trade for gold. Here they found plenty of fish, and fowls, and Indian wine, and bread, for which they gave the people things in exchange. Raleigh says that the Spaniards used to get a hundred pounds of cassava bread for a knife.

There is frequent mention in his narrative of an old king named Topiawari, whose son he brought with him to England. He was a hundred and ten years old, and had been taken prisoner by the Spaniards under Berreo, and led about by them in a chain for seventeen days, that he might guide them from place to place, for he was "a man of great understanding and policy." He purchased his freedom with a hundred plates of gold. This old king came fourteen miles on foot to see the English commander, and returned to his home the same day; which must have been a long journey for one who, as he touchingly observed himself, was "old, weak, and every day called for by death." A number of people came with him from the villages laden with provisions, and amongst these were delicious pine-apples in plenty. One of the people gave Raleigh an armadillo, which he calls "a very wonderful creature, barred all over with small scales, with a horn growing out of it," the powder of which he was told cured deafness.

Raleigh found out, as he thought, where the mines were, and brought some spar with him to England, which was considered to afford satisfactory promise of gold. The old king told him of a mountain of pure gold which Sir Walter believed himself to have seen in the distance; it seemed to him like a white tower, and had a great stream of water flowing over the top of it. But since the rivers had begun to rise, and he had no tools to work the supposed mines with, he resolved to return to England, well pleased that he had found "El Dorado;" and prepared to give a glowing account of the fertility of its soil, its valuable woods and rich gums, its different berries, which dyed the most vivid crimson and carnation hues, its cotton and silk, its pepper, sugar, and ginger, which flourished there as luxuriantly as in the West Indian islands.

Just as the adventurers were about to return to Trinidad, they encountered a terrific storm in the broad mouth of the river Capuri, and were obliged to lie in the dark, close to the shore. At midnight, when the wind began to abate, Raleigh says, "We put ourselves to God's keeping and thrust out into the sea, and left the galley to anchor until daylight. And so, being all very sober and melancholy, one faintly cheering another to show courage, it pleased God that the next day we descried the island of Trinidad."

When Sir Walter arrived in England he published an account of the discovery of the large and beautiful country of Guiana. Either he must have been carried away by the excitement of the adventure, or he must have wilfully exaggerated when he described the gold mines so confidently, since no one who followed him ever found so great a treasure of the precious metal as he declared was in existence. Queen Elizabeth could not be prevailed upon to give orders for the planting of a colony in the new land, much as she desired to increase her dominions, and so it was that the English did not really make a settlement in Guiana until the year 1634.

Raleigh went after his return on a great expedition, which ended in the conquest of Cadiz. In this Essex had the chief command, but it was Raleigh's courage and daring that assured the taking of the city.

The favour he was held in at court now began to decline, and the great fame he had earned as a soldier and a navigator had made him many enemies. It is said that he connived with Cecil for the downfall of Essex, and he was charged by those who bore him ill-will with having taken pleasure in witnessing the execution of that nobleman. His own words, spoken just before his death on the scaffold many years later, will best vindicate him from such an accusation. He said that he was all the time in the armory of the Tower, at the end where he could only just see Essex. He shed tears at his death, and grieved that he was not with him, for he had heard that he had desired to be reconciled with him before he died. And it is natural to suppose that these two men, each one indeed at fault, would have been happier, one in dying and the other while he lived, if they had exchanged a few kind words, at which the old bitterness and hatred would have melted away.

The remaining part of the life of Sir Walter Raleigh was a succession of misfortunes and sorrows: at the death of the queen his good fortune may be said to have deserted him. The same year that James the Sixth of Scotland succeeded his cousin Elizabeth, a plot was formed to place on the throne of England in his stead the Lady Arabella Stuart, who was equally descended from Henry the Seventh with himself. The Lords Grey and Cobham, Sir Walter Raleigh, two Catholic priests, and several others were accused of conniving at it, and arrested for high treason. How far Raleigh was implicated it is difficult now to decide: it is probable that he knew of the plot, because he was the intimate friend of Lord Cobham. He was carried to Winchester, where sentence of death was passed upon him, and he remained there a whole month, daily expecting to be led to the scaffold. At the urgent entreaty of Lady Raleigh the king commuted the sentence of death to imprisonment in the Tower; and there, on the 15th of December, 1603, Raleigh took up his abode, followed by his affectionate wife and his son Walter, who had obtained permission to share his captivity. Most English boys have looked on the rooms in the Tower where this brave man passed more than twelve years, a large portion out of the life on earth, especially on the narrow sleeping-room, to enter which, he had to creep under a low stone archway.

Those years must have contrasted strangely with his past life, full of brave deeds and adventures in a land where all things seemed new. His friends and his enemies alike pitied him now that he was shut up within his gloomy walls. The young Prince Henry had a great regard for him, and admired his brilliant qualities. "Surely," he used to say, "no man but my father would keep such a bird in a cage!"

After his first despair was over he employed himself in making chemical experiments, in educating his children—for his second son Carew was born in the Tower,—and in writing several works, one of which, entitled "The History of the World," has been much admired.

And when, after so many years had passed, and the doors of his prison were opened, he came out into the free air, "a worn, weak, and aged man," almost without fortune, haughty, and prone to take offence no more, but still brave and hopeful. He obtained his liberty chiefly through the interest of the Duke of Buckingham, whose services he paid with the sum of fifteen hundred pounds. He was released on condition of finding the gold mines of Guiana, and having embarked in the enterprise all that remained of his own and his wife's fortunes he set sail for South America, taking with him his son Walter, all the while the sentence of death once passed upon him was still hanging over his head.

But failure and sorrow were in store for him: two of his ships abandoned him; sickness broke out amongst the crews of those that remained, Sir Walter Raleigh was attacked by it himself, and was not able to land when they drew near the shore of Guiana. He deputed Captain Keymis to land with the adventurers, and to repel any Spaniards he might find near the mine. An affray took place in which young Raleigh was killed; and Keymis, attempting to keep a footing on shore, a second time was surprised by some Spaniards who had been lying in wait for him. The failure of the enterprise and the disappointment of Raleigh weighed so heavily upon him, that he killed himself in despair.

Raleigh thus went back to England in sorrow for the loss of his son, and with little hope left that his own life would be spared. When he landed in England he found that the king was very angry with him for having attacked the Spaniards, because he was at peace with their sovereign; and that he intended to renew all his former accusations against him. This King James was led to do by Gondemar, the Spanish ambassador, who bore an extreme hatred to Raleigh; it is even supposed that the Spaniards in Guiana had been secretly told to prepare to resist. James made a proclamation to the effect that he had forbidden all acts of hostility on land belonging to the Spaniards. Directly Raleigh heard this he wrote a letter to the king in defence of his conduct. He was repairing to London, and was met on the road by Sir Lewis Stukely, one of his relations, who told him that he was to arrest him. Then it was that Raleigh yielded to weakness which he repented of in after hours. He pretended that he was ill, that he had lost his reason, anything to delay the moment of his arrest.

Once he planned an escape to France, but when he had got in disguise from the Tower Docks as far as Woolwich he was overtaken by some people in the pay of the Government; and at Greenwich was formally arrested by his kinsman, who had accompanied him in his flight. The next morning, August 7th, he was conducted to the Tower, where he took a kind farewell of the king, and remained imprisoned there until the 28th of October. And on that day, as he was lying ill, the king's officers came at eight o'clock in the morning to convey him to Westminster. Thence he was taken to Gate House, and the next morning to the Old Palace Yard, where the scaffold was erected on which he was to die, that the king might preserve peace with Spain! The people of England thought James was very unkind to condemn a man whose guilt had never been proved, and who was the most valiant and spirited in the whole land. And indeed the execution of Raleigh has ever been considered unjust.

He appeared upon the scaffold with a smiling countenance, and saluted all of his friends and acquaintances who were present. Then he spoke in his own defence, but notwithstanding the deep silence around, his words were not heard by the Lords Arundel and Doncaster, and some other lords and knights who sat at a window looking into the yard, and he begged them to come upon the scaffold. When he had saluted them all he thanked God for having brought him into the light to die, instead of suffering him to die in the dark prison of the Tower. Then he defended himself eloquently against the numerous charges that had been made against him, and ended by entreating all his friends to pray for him, because he said that since he had been a soldier, a captain, a sea-captain, and a courtier, he must needs have fallen into many sins.

The lords and knights departed sorrowfully from the scaffold, and Raleigh prepared for death; he gave away his hat, his wrought night-cap, and some money to some of those who remained near him. "I have a long journey to go," he said, "and therefore I will take my leave." And when he had taken off his black velvet gown and his satin doublet, he called to the headsman, and examined the axe, saying, as he felt along its edge, "This is a sharp medicine, but it is a physician for all disorders." Being asked which way he would lay his head on the block, he said, "So the heart be right, it is no matter which way the head lieth." A minute later his head was severed with two blows from his body; the story of his life was ended, and the unjust king could keep the peace he had purchased with the sacrifice of a man who, although faulty, had many of the attributes of true greatness.

The body of Sir Walter Raleigh was buried in St. Margaret's Church His sorrowing widow kept his head in a case during her lifetime; it wa afterwards buried with her son Carew at West Horsley, in Surrey. Raleig was tenderly attached to his wife, and wrote her an affectionate and solem letter during the early part of his imprisonment, in which he gave her som good advice. "If you can live free from want," he said, "care for no more, fo the rest is but vanity. Love God, and begin betimes; in Him you shall hav everlasting felicity. When you have travelled and wearied yourself with al sorts of worldly cogitations, you shall sit down in sorrow at the end.... Teac your son also to serve and fear God whilst he is young, that the fear of Go may grow up in him."

FOOTNOTES:

[23] This story is mentioned in the "British Biography."

[24] Guiana was originally discovered to the Europeans by Vincent Pinzon before the end of the fifteenth century. It was Juan Martinez, a Spaniard, who first gave the name of El Dorado to the city of Manoa, in Guiana.

[25] A species of palm.

SIR PHILIP SIDNEY

Sir Philip Sidney was born at Penshurst in Kent, in the year 1554. His father, Sir Henry Sidney, was one of the best men that ever lived, and governed Ireland for some time with extreme justice and prudence. His mother was Mary, daughter of the Duke of Northumberland, who was beheaded for maintaining the cause of Lady Jane Grey. She had the sorrow of seeing her brother Lord Guildford Dudley also led to the scaffold; and after these terrible events lived much in retirement, devoting herself to the care and education of her sons Philip and Robert, and her daughter Mary, afterwards Countess of Pembroke.

Under the guidance of such parents, the children at Penshurst grew up in the closest bonds of family love. The grand old house they lived in was an abode worthy of a noble race. It had been given by Edward the Sixth to Sir William Sidney, the grandfather of Sir Philip. The park was famed for its beeches, chestnut trees, and oaks of stately growth; one of the latter, known by the name of "Sidney's Oak," remains standing to this day. Rich pasture lands lay around, the streams abounded with fish, the gardens and orchards with flowers and fruit. Here wandered Sir Philip with his beloved sister, his young brother Robert, who succeeded to his uncle's earldom of Leicester, [26] with the chivalrous Raleigh, the poet Spenser, the play-writer Ben Jonson, and all the good, brave, and clever men of that age.

From his earliest childhood he was so sweet-tempered and intelligent that his father lovingly called him "the light of this family." He was very fond of study, and went first to school at Shrewsbury, where we find he delighted his father greatly, when he was twelve years old, by writing him a letter in Latin, and another in French. At the age of fifteen he went to Christchurch, Oxford, where he appears to have studied with much diligence during the short period of his college life.

In the year 1571 an embassy was sent to the Court of Charles the Ninth of France, in order to treat for a marriage between the king's youngest brother, Henry Duke of Alençon, and Queen Elizabeth. The queen had already shown signs of regard for young Sidney, whom in after years she called "the brightest jewel in her crown," and she allowed him to go abroad with the mission, for the purpose of acquiring a perfect knowledge of foreign languages.

Sir Philip was in Paris on the fatal day of Saint Bartholomew, but was safe in the house of his friend Walsingham, then English minister at the French Court, whilst the unhappy Protestants were being cruelly massacred everywhere around him.

He afterwards travelled through Germany to Vienna, where he made himself perfect in every martial exercise, going thence to study science at Venice, to visit the poet Tasso at Padua, and lastly to Rome.

And whilst he was storing his mind with knowledge, and learning all accomplishments worthy of a true knight, he tried to lead a holy life, and, as far as it was in his power, to keep himself blameless in the sight of God and man; so that when he returned to England at the age of twenty, other men far older than himself looked up to him with respect, and he was considered the brightest ornament of the English Court.

During his travels in Flanders, which at that time belonged to Spain, he had grieved to see how unhappy the people were made by the Duke of Alva, the State minister of Philip the Second of Spain. Philip did not love his Flemish subjects at all; they were mostly Protestants, and he wanted to take their liberty from them and force them to become Roman Catholics. And when they began to rebel against his unjust treatment, he sent the cruel Duke of Alva to them, having first told him that he might do whatever he liked with them.

Alva arrived in Brussels, and began by arresting and imprisoning the Counts Egmont and Horn, two noble-minded men, who, after trying in vain to make peace between the king and the Belgians, had taken the part of the Protestants from a love of justice and mercy. Count Egmont had helped Philip to win the great battle of St. Quentin over the French, but he was compassionate as well as brave, and Philip was so afraid that he would be too kind to the people of Belgium that he advised Alva secretly to get rid of him.

Alva kept the Counts in prison in Ghent for nine months, and then had them carried to Brussels and beheaded, on the 4th of June, 1568, on a scaffold raised on one of the principal squares in the city. They died with courage, martyrs for the liberty of Flanders, but their execution was a cruel injustice, and the people were nearly frantic with grief when the bloody deed was done. Alva remained in Flanders more than four years, and is said to have caused eighteen thousand Protestants to be beheaded during that time. Then Holland rose in revolt; the Prince of Orange was made stadtholder, and Alva, seeing that his day was over, went back to Spain, where he must have been very unhappy when he thought over all his wickedness. The Protestants in Germany fared very little better than those in Flanders, for when the Emperor Rudolf the Second began to reign, he forbade them to worship according to their faith. Sidney was sent on an embassy to Rudolf, and did all he could whilst he was in Germany to humble Spain.

The Flemings asked Elizabeth to be their queen; this she would not agree to, but she sent them some troops and some money, and Sidney implored her to let him take the command in the enterprise, he wanted so much to be of service to his fellow-men, and to deliver those who were unjustly treated from their oppressors. The queen declared, however, that she could not spare him from her Court, and he was obliged to wait patiently a little longer. Meanwhile he took part in the amusements of the Court, the jousts and the royal progresses from place to place, which were always attended with great show. To these must be added the masques, and the first time Sir Philip distinguished himself as an author was by writing a masque, entitled "The Lady of May," which was performed before the queen at Wanstead in Essex. Sidney was the patron of artists, musicians, and authors; he was a kind and sincere friend of the poet Spenser, who had originally been brought from his home in Ireland to the English Court by Sir Walter Raleigh.

Weary at last of remaining inactive, Sidney planned, without the queen's knowledge, an expedition to America, in which he was to be joined by the bold navigator, Sir Francis Drake. He had arrived at Plymouth, whence the ships were to start, when Elizabeth, having gained information of the projected voyage, sent messengers with letters to Sidney, in which she desired him not to sail, and threatened to stay the whole fleet if he did not obey her.

Sir Philip, already on the alert, contrived to intercept the messengers; their letters were taken from them by two soldiers disguised as sailors. The queen, finding threats useless, then sent a positive royal command to her favourite, which he was bound out of duty to his sovereign to obey, and thus he was fated never to see the beautiful new land in the west, with its growth of gorgeous flowers and rich fruits, its giant trees, and its bright-coloured birds, its wonderful landscapes, the beauty of which far exceeded the ideal formed of them.

Elizabeth's displeasure did not last long. It was the high esteem she held him in that made her so loth to let him quit England, and she was not offended with him when he had the courage to write her a letter in which he entreated her not to marry the Duke of Alençon, now Duke of Anjou, and pointed out the trouble such a union might bring upon England. The queen wisely followed his advice, and gave up all idea of a marriage which her subjects had very much disliked.

Sir Philip, one day in the tilt-yard, had a dispute with Lord Oxford, in which both were to blame, but Lord Oxford the more so of the two. This caused Sidney to withdraw for a time from Court, and retire to a house he had at Wilton, where he wrote "The Arcadia," a pastoral romance, and some other works, which gained him the fame of a poet. He did not mean "The Arcadia" to be published, nor did it appear in print until after his death. He wrote it to afford pleasure to his sister Mary, and sent to her each part of it as he completed it.

A time came when the Flemings were again reduced to a state of extreme wretchedness. The great and good stadtholder was basely murdered, and the Spanish troops were making rapid progress through the country. So they asked Elizabeth again to be their queen and to send them succour. She refused the crown a second time, but agreed to help the Flemings with troops on condition that the towns of Flushing and Brille should be placed in her hands. And Sidney, to his great joy, was appointed governor of Flushing, whither he went in November, 1585. The good Count Maurice of Nassau received him as a brother, and he was made general of all the forces, English and Dutch, in the town. Soon he had to welcome there his uncle, the Earl of Leicester, who, by the favour of Elizabeth, was entrusted with the command of the army.

For some time Sidney was obliged to remain inactive, but in the year 1586 he and Count Maurice surprised Axel, a town on the way to Antwerp, and the strongest place held by the Spaniards in the Netherlands. Here he kept his soldiers in the strictest order. When they were marching they were enjoined to be silent, and a band of the choicest among them was stationed in the market-place for the security of the town.

So many brave gentlemen were covetous of the honour of surprising Gravelines, that Sir Philip Sidney, not liking to risk the lives of all, persuaded his inferior officers to try their fortune by dice on the top of a drum. The lot fell upon Sir William Browne, and by this game of hazard [27] the lives of many Englishmen were saved.

On the 30th of August Sidney went with his uncle to invest Doesburg, a fortress on the river Issel. This place was important because it opened the way to Zutphen, and if Zutphen were once taken, the English and Dutch would command the river. Doesburg was gained, and Zutphen soon after surrounded; Leicester guarding it by water, and Sir Philip Sidney, Count Louis of Nassau, and Sir John Norris, guarding it by land.

News was brought to the English camp that a large supply of food was at a place called Deventer, not far off, and Leicester was resolved that it should not be brought into the town, whilst the garrison were equally resolved to receive it. On the morning of the 22nd of September, Sidney advanced to the walls of Zutphen with only 200 men. Before he set out he was clad in complete armour, but meeting the marshal of the camp only lightly armed, he took off some of the armour that covered his legs. There was a mist at the time he set out, but when he had galloped quite close to the town, it dispersed, and he found a thousand of the enemy in readiness to receive him. The fight soon began, his horse was killed under him, and he mounted another. The battle was furious, and the Spaniards, although they were five times as many as the English, were totally routed. In the last charge, Sir Philip was wounded severely in the thigh; his horse, being very mettlesome, rushed furiously from the battle-field, and carried him a mile and a half, wounded and bleeding, to the spot where Leicester stood. When he lay in his anguish on the field, a bottle of water was brought to him that he might quench his thirst; but seeing a soldier near him, wounded like himself, look wistfully at it, he ordered it to be carried to him, saying, "This man's necessity is greater than mine."

His friends and his soldiers were overcome with grief when his state became known; at the sight of his sufferings they almost forgot the glory of his triumph; Yet amidst all his pain, he never ceased declaring that as long as he lived his life was the queen's, and not his own, and that his friends ought not to be discouraged. They laid him gently in his uncle's barge; slowly it glided down the river to Arnheim, in Gelderland, and whilst he lay patiently in it, he was heard to express the hope that his wound was not mortal, and that he might yet have time to become holier before he died.

Day after day he lay in great pain, but talking kindly the while to the friends who grouped lovingly around him, and tended by his wife, Walsingham's daughter, who had hastened to Arnheim as soon as she heard tidings of his disaster. When he felt he could only live a little time longer, he made his confession of Christian faith, and settled his earthly affairs, remembering in his will all those whom he had loved. He took a tender farewell of his brother Robert, telling him "to love his memory and cherish his friends, and to govern his own will by the word of his Creator." And then having called for music, while sweet strains filled the chamber, silent with coming death, the spirit passed from this world.

His remains were brought to England, and interred in the great church of St. Paul, which eighty years later was destroyed by the fire of London.

"Blessed are the dead which die in the Lord:" such were the words inscribed on his coffin; and the perfectness of his character, and the regard in which men held him, cannot be better expressed than in the language of the old chronicle which says, "As his life was most worthie, so his end was most godlie. The love men bore him, left fame behind him; his friendlie courtesie to many procured him good-will of all." [28]

The Poles after the death of their king, Stephen Balori, would have conferred the crown on Sir Philip Sidney, because he was so justly renowned for his humane and upright spirit, but he thought that his first duty was to his sovereign, and the idea was renounced.

FOOTNOTES:

[26] The Earl of Leicester, the Court favourite of Queen Elizabeth, was brother to Lady Mary Sidney.

[27] See "British Biography."

[28] Holinshed.